"Throw away your trendy psycho-pop self-help books. Here, finally, is a practical guide to the process of existential self-affirmation that philosophers tend to lose in a labyrinth of words and systems. Keith Ellis delivers a profound message with wonderful simplicity."

—Dr. James W. Thomasson, former Professor of Theology, Georgetown University

"It's a really wonderful book!"

—David Essel, host of the nationally syndicated talk show *David Essel Alive*

"I really like this book! It's useful and practical and easy to read."

—Ian Punnett, host of the *Ian Punnett* show, WGN in Chicago

"Excellent! One of the most accessible books about goal setting I've ever read."

—Darrell Ankarlo, host of the nationally syndicated *Darrell Ankarlo Show*

"*The Magic Lamp* is a beautifully written and inspirational goal-setting guide that can be appreciated by all age groups. It would be a particularly valuable addition to a professor's 'Recommended Reading' list, and should be made available in libraries and campus bookstores throughout the country."

—Anita Fisher, Ed.D., Professor Emeritus, California State University, Los Angeles

"In *The Magic Lamp*, Keith Ellis presents an intriguing, new, easy-to-follow blueprint for setting and achieving goals by lighting a fire under your wishes and translating them into reality."

—Stephanie Winston, author of *Stephanie Winston's Best Organizing Tips*

"*The Magic Lamp* messages are profound, and it will benefit anyone who reads it. If you apply its principles exactly as suggested, you too will achieve success in all of your endeavors."

—A. Heath Jarrett, Editor, *Jarrett's Journal*

"It's been said that mankind is of three mind sets: those that create, those that understand, and those that neither create nor understand. I think that ignorance exists in the third category, hope in the second, and brilliance in the first. The amount of useful and commonsense advice about goal setting that is contained in *The Magic Lamp* entitles it to automatic entry into the category of brilliance."

—Roger Morrison, Account Manager, Printrak International

"Keith Ellis has made a real breakthrough! He has written the first goal-setting book for the rest of us—not just for success junkies and professional self-improvement types, but for real people facing real problems in a very busy world."

—John W. Leeger, Technical Architect, SAIC

The
Magic Lamp

GOAL SETTING FOR PEOPLE

WHO HATE SETTING GOALS

KEITH ELLIS

THREE RIVERS PRESS

NEW YORK

Published by Three Rivers Press, New York, New York. Member of the Crown Publishing Group.

Random House, Inc. New York, Toronto, London, Sydney, Auckland
www.randomhouse.com

THREE RIVERS PRESS is a registered trademark and the Three Rivers Press colophon is a trademark of Random House, Inc.

Originally published in somewhat different form by Three Waters Press in 1996.

Printed in the United States of America

Library of Congress Cataloging-in-Publication Data
Ellis, Keith.
    The magic lamp : goal setting for people who hate setting goals /
    by Keith Ellis. — 1st ed.
        Originally published: Boston, Va. : Three Waters Press, 1996.
        1. Achievement motivation.   2. Goal (Psychology)   3. Success.
    4. Life skills.   I. Title.
    BF503.E4   1998
    158'.1—dc21   97-44336
                                                           CIP

ISBN 0-609-80166-X

10 9 8

Updated Edition

Disclaimer

The recommendations presented in this book represent the opinions of the Author and do not necessarily represent the opinions of the Publisher. The Reader follows these recommendations at his or her own risk. Neither the Author nor the Publisher makes any warranty of any kind, expressed or implied, about the usefulness, practicality, or safety of any of these recommendations. Neither the Author nor the Publisher assumes any liability whatsoever for the Reader's actions, or consequences of the Reader's actions, whether or not those actions may be said to have been influenced by this book. If you are not willing to comply with these limitations, please do NOT read this book.

To Barbara Gray Ellis,
my mother,
who taught me how
to believe in myself

Contents

Acknowledgments

Unlike someone making a speech at the Oscars, I don't have to pretend that I haven't thought at great length about what I want to say. I have. I owe more than I can express to more good people than I can count. But a few of those people have had such a marked influence on me, and on this book, that I want to thank them by name.

Thanks to Margaret Ellis, my wife, who gave me understanding and support when I disappeared for hours every day to work on *The Magic Lamp*. Then she helped to edit the finished product.

Thanks to Barbara Gray Ellis, my mother, who besides being a great mother and a wonderful human being, is also a fine writer who helped to edit this book.

Thanks to Alan Ellis, my brother, who is the finest wordsmith I know, and one of the most inspirational thinkers. Time after time he came up with great ideas for what I should say in this book, and how I should say it, then let me claim the credit for his thoughts as if they were my own.

Finally, thanks to all the writers and thinkers, the speakers and doers I have studied for all these years. Many of them are listed in the Resources section at the back of this book. Many more are not. To all of them I offer my humble gratitude. When you stand on the shoulders of giants, it's easy to see the sky.

Author's Note: On the Use of Personal Pronouns

In much of what is written in the English language, the masculine pronouns *he, him,* and *his* refer to persons of both sexes. Many women take exception to this. Many men would too, if it worked the other way around. There are two ways to fix this problem: We can change the language, or we can change ourselves. I prefer the latter. Only then will the language follow.

Let us rid personal pronouns of their political significance and thereby deny them the power to divide us. Let male writers use masculine pronouns, and we shall understand nothing more than that these writers are men. Let female writers use feminine pronouns, and we shall understand nothing more than that these writers are women. Let readers see past the pronoun to the writer. When the gender of a pronoun signifies nothing more than the gender of the writer—instead of the gender of reality—we will all be on the right path.

Introduction

In 1921, Dr. Lewis Terman of Stanford University began a land-mark study of 1,528 gifted children, all of whom had an IQ above the level of genius. The objective was to better understand the relationship between human intelligence and human achievement. This study became world famous and continued for decades, producing some of the most remarkable insights into the role that intelligence plays in a successful life.

But the most remarkable insight of all was that IQ is not the most important ingredient for success. Instead, Terman's study found that three factors are far more important than sheer intelligence when it comes to achievement: self-confidence, perseverance, and a tendency to set goals. The most important of all—even for geniuses—is the tendency to set goals.

I was not part of the Terman study—I'm no genius—but for some reason I've always been interested in the process of setting goals. I find it particularly fascinating that so many people talk about the power of setting goals, but so few people ever seem to set them.

I was a perfect example. For years I read every book on goal setting that I could lay my hands on. I listened to every audio-cassette about goal setting I could beg, borrow, or buy. I attended every seminar about goal setting that came to town, and traveled to many that never made it to town. I knew everything there was to know about setting goals. I just never set any.

For one thing, goals bored me. For another, they threatened me. They locked me in a cage when all I wanted was the freedom to be open to every opportunity, but the obligation to pursue none. I knew that goals worked, but I was never willing to put them to work.

Then in the shower one morning I was daydreaming about the fame and fortune I would possess if only I could make my wishes come true—like in a fairy tale. What a wonderful fantasy! Too bad there was a catch—in a fairy tale you could always count on a fairy godmother for help, or a wizard, or a genie. Unfortunately, all I could count on was myself.

That got my attention. What if I really could count on myself? What if I could figure out exactly what I wanted from life and then make it happen? What if making a wish come true was as easy as setting a goal?

BINGO!—I had finally struck brain!

Wishes *are* goals—but goals with snap, crackle, and pop. Goals provide the process that can take you anywhere you want to go, but they lack the inspiration to get you there. Wishes are different. They have impact—like being struck by lightning instead of by a lightning bug. They let you dream. They let you soar. They let you tap into a source of limitless possibility and boundless energy that gives you the power to accomplish what you might otherwise never even have imagined. If you want to make good things happen in your life, think in terms of wishes instead of goals.

I was so excited I nearly slipped on a bar of soap. Wishing was the answer I'd been seeking for years. I never felt much joy in rolling out of bed in the morning and telling myself, "Today I'm going to work on my goals." But the thought of saying, "Today I'm going to make my wishes come true"—that got me excited. That made me feel as though I could accomplish anything. It was the missing spark that could set my life ablaze with success, prosperity, and happiness.

I stepped out of the shower, grabbed a notepad, and began writing as fast as I could, trying to capture all the ideas that poured out of me faster than my hand could drag a pen across the paper. In the weeks that followed I transformed everything I knew about goal setting into a strategy for wishing. I named this strategy the L.A.M.P. Process. As soon as I committed my ideas to paper, I put them to work. As soon as I put them to work, I began to make my wishes come true.

The L.A.M.P. Process catapulted me from the minor leagues of achievement to the major leagues of success. I can't say it happened overnight—it didn't take that long. The moment I changed me, the world changed around me. The things I wanted to happen, began to happen. The kind of life I had been afraid even to dream about began to unfold before my eyes—like magic.

I've written *The Magic Lamp* to share with you this remarkable power to make your wishes come true. My intent is to offer a strategy, not a sermon. I'm not going to preach about motivation or try to sell you on success. I assume that you already want more from life than what you have and you're searching for a way to get it. That's exactly what you'll find here: a way to get it, whatever your background, whatever your age, whatever your circumstances.

But what about luck? Isn't it true that fortune—good or ill—is what ultimately determines our fate?

Luck performs its part in what happens to you; what you'll learn here is how to perform yours. Fortune deals the cards; what you'll learn here is how to play them. Fate rules, but favors those who learn the rules. This book is about the most important rule of all—*cause and effect*.

Cause and Effect

Have you ever run a stoplight and not been given a ticket? You were lucky. You got away with it. Have you ever jumped from a ten-story building and not been hurt? Don't try it. You won't get lucky. You won't get away with it. You may be able to break the laws of man, and from time to time you may even get away with it, but you can't break the laws of nature. If you try, they will only break you.

Consider the law of cause and effect. For every effect there must be a cause. That cause must always precede the effect. Simple, direct, inescapable, it's perhaps the easiest natural law to remember—and it is definitely the easiest to forget.

Who would stand in front of a woodstove and demand heat without first filling the stove with wood? No one in his right mind. But how often have you heard someone swear that from now on he will do only what he is paid to do—and nothing more—unless he gets a raise? The law of cause and effect says he'll have a long wait. He must first do more than he is being paid for, to make himself worth more than he is being paid.

Who would expect to make a withdrawal from a savings

account before first making a deposit? No one in his right mind. But have you ever had a friend who demanded more from a relationship without first being willing to invest more in that relationship? Because of the law of cause and effect, this kind of person will always be in for a big disappointment.

Who would stand before a patch of barren earth and demand vegetables without first planting a garden? No one in his right mind. But have you ever met someone who feels entitled to the rewards of success without first being willing to invest the time and effort it takes to become successful? According to the law of cause and effect, the investment must always come first, if the rewards are to follow.

Life teaches us that we have to put wood in a woodstove *before* we get heat; we have to make a deposit *before* we can make a withdrawal; we have to plant seeds, water them, weed them, and nurture them *before* we can harvest our first ear of corn or pick our first tomato. Too often, we don't apply this knowledge to the way we run our lives.

If you desire a specific effect in your life—whether it involves a relationship, or a job, or an important project—you must *first* set in motion the cause of that effect. Whenever that cause is missing, the effect will be missing as well. Whenever the effect is missing, you can be certain that you have neglected to set in motion the appropriate cause.

You can be equally certain that once you set in motion that cause, the effect you desire will follow—without fail—as reliably as the sun chases the first glimmer of dawn over the horizon. The cause must always come first. Once it does, you can count on the effect.

One of the most important decisions you will ever make in

life is this: *Do you choose to be a cause or an effect?* When you choose to be a cause, you make things happen. When you choose to be an effect, you settle for whatever happens to you.

When you choose to be a cause, you become the star quarterback of your own life, the Most Valuable Player of your own Super Bowl. When you choose to be an effect, you just watch from the stands. You're content to laugh and to cry, to live and to die, based on the actions of others.

The difference between being a cause and being an effect is the difference between being a hammer and being a nail. One acts; the other is acted upon. *The Magic Lamp* presents a strategy for those who would rather be a hammer than a nail.

The L.A.M.P. Process

The Magic Lamp will show you how to set in motion the causes that will produce the effects you want. I call this the L.A.M.P. Process. The letters *L*, *A*, *M*, and *P* each stand for one of the four major steps in the process. You can memorize these steps in less than a minute and apply them for the rest of your life. When you're done with this book, you will understand why you don't need iron-willed self-discipline to be successful. You will understand why you don't need to be particularly talented or intelligent to make your wishes come true. You just need to follow these four steps:

Step 1. Lock On

> *Decide what you want to wish for. Think of it as choosing the effect you wish to cause. Once you have chosen that effect, lock on it the way a guided missile locks on its target.*

Step 2. A̲ct

> *Set in motion the causes that will make your wish come true.*

Step 3. M̲anage your progress

> *Track the causes you've set in motion to make sure that they are producing the effects you want. If they aren't, then adjust what you're doing.*

Step 4. P̲ersist

> *Finish what you start.*

A crowbar is a tool that works according to the principle of leverage. The L.A.M.P. Process is a tool that works according to the principle of cause and effect. In both cases, the principle is what counts, not the tool. The principle is what makes things happen; the tool is merely the instrument. The next book you read may teach you a better tool than the L.A.M.P. Process, but you will never find a better principle than this one:

> *To get whatever you want from life you have only to set in motion the appropriate cause, and the effect will take care of itself.*

Lock this in your mind for now. It will open the entire world to you later.

L.A.M.P. Process Step 1:

_Lock On

1 What Do You Want?

I am master of earth and air and wave,
but slave of the lamp and the bearer's slave.
What will you have, Master, what will you
have?

THE GENIE OF THE LAMP
ONE THOUSAND AND ONE ARABIAN NIGHTS

Imagine taking a stroll one balmy evening when, in the twilight, you stumble across an ancient brass lamp, the kind you might expect to find in a Turkish bazaar. You stoop to retrieve the lamp and notice in the dimness an inscription carved along one side. Centuries of tarnish and neglect make the writing almost illegible, so you buff it two or three times with your sleeve.

KA-WHAM! The lamp erupts in a blast of smoke and flame. Stumbling backward, you drop the lamp and shield your eyes. When you open them again, standing before you, as big as a billboard, is a genie.

He looks at you with a gleam in his eye. And with a voice that rolls in like thunder from the horizon, he says, "I am the Genie of the Lamp. What will you have, Master, what will you have?"

What would you ask the genie to do?

Believe it or not, you own just such a lamp. It is located about a centimeter behind your eyeballs, right between your ears. And medical science has even given it a name. It's called the human brain. It is the most powerful computer on earth. In fact, it is so powerful that it has invented all the other computers on earth. It has invented everything from supercomputers to moon landings to sliced bread.

And you own such a brain, free and clear. Yours is the equal of any other brain on the planet. You are its sole proprietor, the only one who can summon forth its awesome power to make your wishes come true. You are literally your own genie, brimming with the godlike power of creation. Congratulations!

But that still leaves you with the same problem, doesn't it? What will you ask the genie to do?

Before you can make your wishes come true, you must first decide what to wish for. When people don't get what they want from life, usually it's because they don't know what they want. They grind through one work week after another, daydreaming about the good life, but they rarely muster a clear idea of what that "good life" should be. As competent and hardworking as they are, they lack purpose. They've been taught how to shoot, but they've never been taught how to aim.

Perhaps the most startling truth about human nature is that anyone can do something truly remarkable in life if he or she has something truly remarkable to do. Once you decide what you really want, the rest falls into place. You awaken each morning with a reason to get out of bed. Your days are filled with meaning because you fill them with meaningful work. You are able to take advantage of your talents, your time, and your opportunities because you have a purpose. Without this purpose the astonishing power you have to grant your own wishes sits idle, double-parked, the motor running with no one behind the wheel. But with this purpose, you shift smoothly through the gears, traveling at speeds far beyond your comprehension.

So go ahead, slip into the driver's seat. Figure out what you really want—not what you're supposed to want, not what someone else wants for you, but what you in your heart of hearts want for yourself.

Brainstorming

The easiest way to find out what you really want is to ask yourself. Specifically, ask your subconscious mind, the powerhouse of your intellect. This is where your deepest and best thinking is done. The quality of the answers you receive will depend on how you ask your questions, so I suggest you use a tool that is designed specifically to help you tap the power of your subconscious mind. This tool is called *brainstorming*. I've outlined how it works in five steps below:

> *1. Write the topic you want to brainstorm in the form of a question at the top of a clean sheet of paper.*

The human mind is the most powerful computer on earth, but you don't have to learn a programming language to use it; all you have to do is to ask it a question.

2. Write whatever pops into your head.

Ask yourself the question you've written at the top of your page, then listen to your answers—all your answers. The best way to listen is to write your answers down. Write every thought that floats into your mind when you ask your question. Write the silly thoughts. Write the painful ones. Write the thoughts that embarrass you, even the ones that seem to make no sense. You aren't going to share this list with anyone, so write everything that pops into your mind, whether it seems useful or not, whether you approve of it or not. The first rule of brainstorming is to listen to yourself. If you don't, who will?

3. Accept with gratitude whatever pops into your head.

No matter how silly your thoughts may seem, no matter how impossible, or preposterous, or embarrassing, remind yourself how fortunate you are to have so many interesting ideas.

Think of each idea as a gift. We might not like every gift we receive, but we accept each one, we open each one, and we thank the giver. It's the thought that counts. If you accept all your thoughts gratefully, your subconscious—like any other giver of gifts—will be that much more willing to keep them coming.

4. Keep your pen moving.

Tell yourself you're going to write for a fixed amount of time—a minute, two minutes, five minutes—and then keep your pen moving until the time is up. Keep writing even if what you write seems like nonsense. Keep writing even if you have to write the same thing over and over. Keep writing, and sooner or later you will discover you have something to say.

5. Save your criticism for later.

Write, don't judge. You can judge later. Brainstorming is a tool to generate ideas, not to evaluate them.

Have you ever offered a suggestion in a meeting, only to have someone point out how stupid it was? After that, you probably learned to keep your thoughts to yourself.

Your subconscious is just as sensitive. If you reject its suggestions, it stops making them. It's like a faucet—either it's turned on or it's turned off. The purpose in brainstorming is to turn the faucet on full blast and keep it on. Generate as many ideas as you can. Let your writer flow, and let your editor go. You can sort it all out later.

There is no time like the present to begin your first official brainstorming session. So take out a blank sheet of paper and write this question at the top:

> *What would I really want from life if I were absolutely, positively certain I would get it?*

Now write your answers. Don't worry about how you're going to accomplish the things on your list; we'll deal with that later. For now, focus on what you want, not on how you'll get it.

Write whatever pops into your mind. Keep your pen moving for at least two minutes. You might find it helpful to think about specific areas of your life. For example, what do you want from your work? From your home life? From your relationships? What kind of health do you want? What kind of physique? What do you want from your hobbies? From your community activities? From your love life? What kind of impact would you like to have on the world? With whom would you like to associate? How would you like to be remembered?

If you run out of steam, write the same answers over and over, each time with a slightly different twist. Change a word, change a color or a size, change an adjective. Whatever you do, keep writing for at least two minutes—longer if the ideas keep flowing. Go ahead, write.

Once you've completed this little bit of brainstorming, try the same thing with a slightly different question:

> *What would I really want to accomplish in life if I were absolutely, positively certain I would do it?*

You may find that you come up with a very different set of answers from the ones that came to you as a result of the first question.

When you're done with this two-part brainstorming exercise, take a break. Stand and stretch; go to the bathroom; take a walk; at the very least, draw a few deep breaths. When you come back, you're going to switch gears, and you'll need to feel fresh enough to take on a new challenge.

Priorities

You have just created your first honest-to-goodness *wish list*. Actually, you've created two lists, so merge them into one. At this stage in your wishing career, it's a good idea to work on only one wish at a time, so you need to decide which item on your combined list you want to work on first. Here's how you go about it.

The first thing you do is to number the items on your combined list. Then look at items 1 and 2. Which is more important to you? In your mind, label that item the *Current Choice.* Then move to the next item on your combined list—number 3—and compare it with your Current Choice. Which of them is more important to you? The one you prefer becomes your Current Choice. Now move to the next item on your list—number 4— and compare that with your Current Choice. Which of them is more important to you? The one you prefer becomes your Current Choice.

Repeat this process for each item on your list, comparing each one with whatever your Current Choice happens to be at that moment. Whenever you prefer a new item over your Current Choice, then that new item becomes your Current Choice. Continue until you've gone through your entire list.

When you come to the end of your list, the Current Choice that remains is the single most important item on your list. It has become your *First Choice.* You have compared it directly or indirectly with every other item and preferred it every time. Now write a big "#1" beside it. It's the first wish you're going to make come true, the wish you're going to work on for the rest of this book.

This process of setting priorities is called a "bubble sort" because it allows the most important item to rise to the top of your list, the way bubbles rise to the top of a glass of champagne. I like it because it allows me to reduce even the most complicated decisions to a series of simple choices between two alternatives.

Even when I'm trying to prioritize a long list of items, I never have to compare more than two items at a time. You'll find it a handy tool whenever you have a choice to make, so you might want to practice it some more before you move on.

Go ahead and rank the second most important item on your wish list. Ignore your First Choice because you've already ranked it. Instead, consider the remaining items, comparing only two at a time, the same way you worked through the list the first time. When you're done with the second pass, you will have selected your *Second Choice*—the second most important item on your list. Put "#2" beside it. Repeat the process to discover your *Third Choice,* your *Fourth Choice,* and so on, until you've ranked the top ten items on your list.

Tough Choices

What happens when you can't make up your mind between *A* or *B?* Assume for the moment that you can't have both; either it's one or none. Ask yourself, what would it feel like living without *A?* Listen to your answer. Then ask yourself, what it would feel like living without *B?* If a little voice inside you says it would be easier to live without one than to live without the other, take the hint. You've made your decision.

When you absolutely, positively can't decide between two alternatives, flip a coin. I'm serious. If you really can't choose between them, then it doesn't matter which one you choose, does it? They must be pretty close to equal, so why not make it easy on yourself?

If you do make a decision by flipping a coin, don't be surprised if you hear a little voice inside that says you made the wrong choice. Perhaps your options weren't as equal as you thought. That's OK—you can always change your mind. At least the coin flip got you off the fence.

Remember, at this point all you're doing is establishing priorities. You aren't discarding any options. You're just choosing which wish to work on first, then second, then third. Once you've made that decision, you simply carry out your wishes in the order of their importance to you.

But first you must see how your wish helps you fulfill your purpose in life.

2 *Purpose*

Rumor has it that a philosopher in Europe once posted this message on his telephone answering machine:

> *"This device is programmed to ask two simple questions: Who are you and what do you want? Most people live their entire lives without ever answering either one."*

The people who are most successful at making their wishes come true are the people who know who they are and what they want. They choose wishes that help them fulfill their purpose in life. To make the most of your astonishing power to make your wishes come true, the first thing you need to do is to choose a purpose, and then choose wishes that will help you fulfill that purpose.

Earl Nightingale, one of the great modern philosophers of human achievement, used to distinguish between *river people* and *goal people*. He said that river people are those lucky few who seem to be born for a particular purpose. From the time they are children they seem to know what they are meant to do with their lives. They find themselves in the middle of a great river of interest, and they flow with that river all the days of their lives.

Then there are the rest of us. We are the goal people or, more appropriately for this book, we are the *wish* people. We aren't born with an all-consuming interest. We aren't born into our purpose in life. Instead, we have to define it.

I certainly wasn't born with a river of interest. For decades, I wondered what I was supposed to do with my life. I envied people who knew what they were about, people who seemed to have been born with a sense of mission, people who were fortunate enough to pursue their river of interest. If only that could happen to me, I used to tell myself. And then one afternoon, it did.

I was walking in the woods—I can still remember the exact spot—and wondering what I was going to do with my life. Suddenly, I had the answer. As clearly as if it had been engraved on my forehead, I understood that my great purpose in life was to define my purpose. *That* was my mission. *That* was my river of interest. And it always had been. For my entire adult life, I had been pursuing the same mission—to define my purpose. But I had never realized it. I had never acknowledged it as a mission. I had never accepted it as a valid purpose. Once I did, I understood with absolute certainty what it was that I was supposed to do with my life: I was put on earth to define my purpose.

For the first time in my life, I felt like a river person. I knew what my life was about. I had a reason to get out of bed in the morning. My days were filled with meaning because I had suddenly filled them with meaningful work. I had something vitally important to accomplish—a purpose—and I couldn't wait to get started on it each day.

What I learned that day is that it doesn't matter what purpose you have. It simply matters that you have one. And if you don't have one, then your purpose is to define one. That becomes your river of interest.

Once you adopt this frame of mind, you will find that everything else falls into place. You will embark on a journey of self-discovery. You will open yourself to new thoughts, activities, and interests that you would never have considered before. Everything you do from that moment on will become part of your newly discovered purpose, your newly discovered mission in life: to define—to invent—yourself.

To find your purpose, start with what interests you. I've never met anyone who didn't have an interest in something. But I've met many people who have never allowed themselves to acknowledge their interests. They feel that the things they like to do are unimportant in the great scheme of things, so they look elsewhere for meaning and purpose. Meanwhile, what they are looking for is right under their nose.

Finding your purpose in life doesn't have to be some grandiose quest. Instead of asking, "What do I want to do with my life?" why not make it easy on yourself? Ask, "What do I enjoy doing?" Then listen to your answers—*all* of your answers. Write them on a piece of paper. Write everything you can think of. Write the trivial things. Write the silly things. Write the embarrassing things. Write whatever pops into your mind. You don't have to share these ideas with anyone. You simply have to share them with yourself. If what interests you doesn't seem important enough to put on paper, that's only because you're trying to judge your interests instead of trying to live them. Try living them, instead, and you'll take your first great step toward making your wishes come true.

If you enjoy doing something, do it. Do you like to listen to music, go to the movies, read, watch TV, cook, work on cars, learn, clean house, take walks, watch birds, teach, carve soap, build furniture, sew, surf the Net, write poetry, build sand castles? As long as your activity or hobby is not self-destructive (like substance abuse), hurtful to someone else, or damaging to the environment, why not allow yourself to enjoy it for all it's worth?

If you enjoy something, pursue it. You don't have to make it your official purpose in life—but what if you did? What if you decided to spend your life doing what you enjoy? That's what river people do. Sometimes they're called eccentric, or absent-minded, or obsessive. Sometimes they're called geniuses. But whatever they're called, all they do is flow with their river of interest and allow themselves to enjoy the journey. They don't care if what they're doing is important to the rest of the world; they care if it's important to them. They aren't out to save mankind; they're out to save themselves—from a life without joy or meaning.

But isn't that selfish? You bet it is. It's the good kind of selfish, the enlightened kind, the kind that says you will bring far more good to the world by doing what you care about than by doing what you hate. If you want to maximize your contribution to your fellow human beings, you owe it to them, and to yourself, to follow your dreams, to follow your purpose, to follow your bliss.

Do what you think you're meant to do, not what you think you're supposed to do. If you're worried that you'll never amount to much unless your purpose is "worthy," don't waste your time. You already amount to something. Your achievements in life are not the source of your worth as a human being; they are the result of it. Self-worth comes before purpose, not the other way around. Once you accept your value as a person, once you accept that you already amount to something, then you free yourself to make the most of your life. You free yourself to define your purpose. And that's where the fun begins.

Finding your purpose is a matter of asking yourself what you enjoy doing, and then doing it. That's what river people do. They aren't making a huge sacrifice to follow their dreams. They don't have to practice iron-willed self-discipline to keep themselves on track. They simply do what they enjoy doing. That's their payoff. That's why they do it. Their achievements are simply a by-product of that enjoyment.

Once you define a purpose—even if that purpose is simply to define a purpose—the rest will take care of itself. Your life will take on a focus and intensity of which you've never dreamed. One by one you will begin to make your wishes come true. Day by day you'll find yourself growing, contributing more to those around you, and making the most of yourself as a human being. That is the noblest purpose of all.

3 Are You Willing to Pay the Price?

Take whatever you want, said God, but pay for it.

OLD SPANISH PROVERB

There was once a cocktail party at which a world-famous pianist gave a recital. After the performance, the hostess said to the pianist, "I would give anything to be able to play like you."

The pianist looked at her thoughtfully for a moment and replied, "No, you wouldn't."

The hostess, surprised and embarrassed in front of her guests, said, "I most certainly would."

The pianist shook his head. "You would love to play as I play now, but you are not willing to practice eight hours a day for the next twenty years to learn how to play that way."

The room was silent as the guests stared into their plates. There was no debate. They knew the pianist was right. The hostess was bluffing. She wanted to *be* a concert pianist, but she wasn't willing to pay the price to *become* one.

Every wish has its price. You can have anything you want if you are willing to pay that price. The price may be in dollars and cents. Or it may be in effort—the weeks or months or years it will take you to make your wish come true. Or the price may be in sacrifice, what you have to give up in order to get what you want. Whatever the price turns out to be, you have to pay full retail—you can't bargain with fate.

Your willingness to pay the price is what gives you the power to cause your wish to come true. If you are 100 percent willing to pay the price, then you are 100 percent likely to succeed. If you are only 50 percent willing to pay the price, then you are 50 percent likely to succeed. It's a simple matter of cause and effect. The price is the cause; the wish is the effect. Pay the price—set in motion the appropriate cause—and the wish will take care of itself.

A Compelling Reason

Take a look at the First Choice from your wish list. How much will it cost you? How much will it cost in dollars and cents? How much will it cost in effort? How many weeks or months or years will you have to work on it? How much will it cost in sacrifice? Will it mean less time with your family, less time with your friends, less time watching TV, less time with your hobby, or playing golf, or puttering around the house? Once you have an idea of what that wish will cost, are you willing to pay the price?

Now here is an interesting question: Why are you willing to

pay that price? What reasons do you have to make that wish come true?

The people who are most successful at making their wishes come true are the ones who have the most compelling reasons to do so. Instead of trying to psyche yourself into paying an exorbitant price for a wish, why not choose a wish that is worth the price in the first place? Choose a wish that compels you to make it come true.

If your First Choice doesn't compel you, choose another wish. Go to your Second Choice or your Third Choice. Redo your wish list if you have to. Brainstorm new ideas and set new priorities until you choose a wish that compels you to pay the price, a wish that makes it more than worth your while to overcome every obstacle that will stand in your way. Choose a wish that is so compelling, you refuse to settle for less. You're not going to get very far until you do.

Growth

While you are looking for a compelling wish, keep this in mind: Choose a wish for what it will make of you to achieve it. The greater the wish, the greater you have to become to make that wish come true. That's the real payoff. That's why human beings strive for more than what they have. It's not what you achieve that brings you joy and fulfillment; it's the person you must become in order to achieve it. You don't get what you want from life; you get what you are.

That's why it takes effort to make your magic lamp work. If all you had to do were to snap your fingers to get anything you want, you would never have to develop your potential. You would never have to become more than what you are. But by insisting that the only way to earn your wish is to become the kind of person for whom such a wish is possible, the universe gives you one of the greatest gifts of all: *growth*.

Along with this gift comes a warning: Beware any wish that turns you into someone you don't want to be. That price is too high. No wish is worth sacrificing your values, your character, or your integrity. No wish is worth losing the only things worth having. If a wish forces you to become less of a person than you want to be, it's not worth the price.

4 Make Your Wish Presentable

Wishing gets a lot of bad press. As kids we're told, "If wishes were horses beggars would ride." What a crock! If beggars knew how to wish, they could charter a limousine.

Wishing has been at the heart of human accomplishment since our ancestors first dropped from the trees and began to pad along the path toward civilization. Wishing is the most powerful force at our command. But most of us don't know it exists, let alone how to command it.

The secret is this: Don't just make a wish; make it *presentable*. The power of your wish comes from the way you present it to your conscious and subconscious. If you present it effectively, you will harness the genie-like power of your mind and cause your wish to come true. If you present it ineffectively, your mind will shrug it off as just another one of those good intentions, ill-timed and unachievable.

Below are eleven steps that will help you make your wish so presentable that your mind will just naturally make it come true. As you read each step, apply it to the wish you have decided to work on first.

1. Write it.

If you think your wish is fixed so clearly in your mind that you don't have to put it on paper, you're kidding yourself. Write it, or kiss it good-bye. When you write your wish, you give it the kind of clarity, focus, and urgency that you can't give it any other way. You hang it out there in the world right in front of your eyes. You turn it into something real, something that stares back at you from the page and dares you to make it come true.

If you want to make your wish come true, write it down. If you don't want to make it come true, then don't write it down. If it's not written, then it's not a wish—period.

2. Be specific.

A presentable wish is specific down to the last detail. When you can picture precisely what you want—when you can feel it, hear it, touch it, smell it, and taste it—that's specific.

The more specific you are, the better your chances for getting what you want. If you want money, how much money? by when? If you want a new house, what kind of house? where? how many rooms? If you want a better job, in what field? at what pay? for what company? If you want a richer relationship, with whom? what will it feel like? sound like? look like?

When you make your wish specific, you give yourself a host of powerful advantages:

• You can track your progress.

If you don't know what you want, how will you know when you get it? For that matter, how do you know you don't already have it?

• You avoid ambiguity.

If you say, "I wish for either *A* or *B*," then your mind can't tell which alternative you want it to focus on, so it won't focus on either. But if you concentrate on a single specific wish, you free your mind to act without restraint or confusion.

• You avoid unintended results.

Vague wishes can be dangerous because they can be granted in unintended ways. For example, if you wish for "more freedom at work," you might find yourself fired. If you wish to "lose weight," you might find yourself with a serious illness, one symptom of which is weight loss. If you wish for "lots of money," you might find yourself the beneficiary of a large life-insurance policy, but the person you love the most had to die for you to collect it. Wish for exactly what you want, and you won't find yourself with what you don't want.

• You focus your brainpower.

Have you ever noticed that you tend to pay attention to the things you're interested in? You buy a new car, and you begin to notice how many other people are driving the same car. You fall in love with a redhead, and you begin to notice how many other people have red hair. You read a book about nature, and you begin to notice the sunsets and the songbirds, though both have been there all along.

When you're specific about what you want, you alert your brain to notice all the people, information, and resources that can help you cause your wish to come true. Everywhere you look, you discover helpful coincidences—what the rest of the world calls *luck*—but these are coincidences you have made possible by being aware of exactly what you want. The more specific you are, the more luck you will create.

3. Set a deadline.

A wish without a deadline is just an idle daydream, with no beginning and no end. A deadline imparts a sense of urgency, the way you feel when you're about to leave town. But a deadline isn't meant to make you panic, it's meant to make you focus. Don't wear it like a straitjacket. If you find you're going to miss a deadline, go ahead and change it. Be comfortable with it. But keep your eye on it. If you want to make your wish come true, know exactly what you're shooting for—and when.

4. Make it something you can measure.

You can be winning and think you're losing because you aren't keeping score. Measurement is your way of keeping score. Measurement lets you see how much progress you have already made and how far you have to go. If you can't measure your wish, you won't know when you've made it come true.

Some wishes are easy to measure, such as making a certain amount of money or losing a certain amount of weight. But how do you wish for things that aren't measurable, such as a better marriage, or a more satisfying job, or a sense of inner peace? It's easy—just turn those wishes into something you can measure. Turn them into specific actions.

For example, suppose your wish is to have a better marriage. To turn this unmeasurable wish into something you can measure, ask yourself these questions:

1. What specific changes can I make in the way I act toward my partner in order to improve our marriage?
2. Will I make these changes all at once or gradually?
3. By what date will I complete them?

Once you have identified specific measurable actions you can take to improve your marriage, you can phrase your wish in terms of these actions. For instance, instead of wishing for a better marriage, which you can't measure, you might wish to rub your partner's back a couple of nights a week. You might wish to vacuum the house once a month instead of letting your partner do all the housework. You might wish to cut the grass every other week instead of letting your partner do all the yard work. You might wish to take the kids to soccer practice on Saturday mornings so your partner can sleep late. You might wish to take out the garbage, or wrap the birthday presents, or clean up after a dinner party—anything to lighten the load on your partner and sweeten the relationship.

The same approach applies to wishing for a state of mind, such as happiness, joy, or contentment. You can't measure these things, so wish instead for the specific actions that will lead to the state of mind you want.

For example, if you wish to feel inner peace, and you feel it most when you're on a camping trip, wish to spend more time camping. If you wish to feel fulfilled, and you feel it most when you're performing community service, wish to spend more time serving your community. If you wish to feel happy, and you feel it most when you're with your family, wish to spend more time with your family.

Wish for something you can measure, and you will consistently measure success.

5. Wish only for what you can control.

A wish is about what you do—not what anyone else does—because that's the only thing you can control. There is no place in your wish for what you want someone else to think, or do, or feel, because you can't make those things happen. Concentrate instead on the things you can make happen.

For instance, you can't wish to be loved, because you can't make that happen. But you can wish to be loving. You can't wish for that heartthrob next door to go to dinner with you, because you can't make that happen. But you can wish for the courage to ask that person to dinner. You can't wish for someone else to make you happy, because you can't make that happen. But you can wish to spend more of your time doing the things that make you happy.

If you wish only for what you can control, then success will always be in your hands. If you wish for something you can't control, then success will always be in the hands of someone else.

6. Wish for what you want, not what you don't want.

Your mind moves you toward whatever you think about. If you think about what you want, you'll move toward it. If you think about what you don't want, you'll move toward that instead.

Rather than saying, *"I wish I wasn't broke,"* tell yourself, *"I choose to have $100,000 in the bank."*

Rather than saying, *"I wish I wasn't fat,"* tell yourself, *"I choose to lose thirty pounds."*

Rather than saying, *"I wish I wasn't stupid,"* tell yourself, *"I choose to educate myself."*

Rather than saying, *"I wish I didn't slice my tee shot,"* tell yourself, *"I choose to hit my tee shot straight as an arrow."*

Rather than saying, *"I wish I wasn't so lonely,"* tell yourself, *"I choose to make some friends."*

Ask for what you want, and you'll get it. Ask for what you don't want, and you'll be stuck with that instead.

7. Begin your wish with "I choose."

The real secret to success is not self-discipline; it's choosing to succeed. The moment you make a choice, you eliminate all the doubt and hesitation that exist when you're trying to make up your mind. Instead of worrying about what to do, you just do it. You throw a little switch in your brain that commands you to do whatever it takes to carry out your decision. You summon all the powers of your body and mind to execute your choice.

A wish is a choice set in motion. The most effective way to set a choice in motion is to begin a wish with the words *"I choose."* These words then transform your wish into a powerful command to carry out whatever you have chosen to do. Whenever you say *"I choose,"* you choose success.

8. Make it emotional.

Your wish should include an emotional payoff so you can use the power of that emotion to help you cause your wish to come true. For instance, if your wish is to improve your marriage, you might say, "I choose to *lovingly* help my partner with the chores." If your wish is to get up each morning at six, to give yourself some personal time before you go to work, you might say, "I choose to *cheerfully* rise each morning at six." If your wish is to increase company revenues by 50 percent, you might say, "I choose to *joyfully* increase company revenues by 50 percent."

I can go into a lot of psychological mumbo jumbo about why this is important, but instead of telling you about it, I would rather show you. Play along with me and you'll see what I mean.

Choose an emotion you would like to feel when you make your wish come true. Now, add that word to your wish. For instance, if joy is what you want to feel, and your wish is "I choose to find a new job," change your wish so that it reads, "I choose to *joyfully* find a new job. Then say your wish aloud, with the emotion word included, and make sure you feel the emotion when you say it. If you're saying "cheerful," *feel* cheerful. If you're saying "happy," *feel* happy. If you're saying "triumphant," *feel* triumphant.

Now remove the emotion word and repeat your wish without any emotion at all. Notice how flat it feels. It's no longer charged with passion or spirit. Your wish is like an electrical appliance, and your emotions are like a wall socket. You'll get a lot more done if you stay plugged in.

When you build an emotional payoff into your wish, you tend to work harder at it because you enjoy it more. The harder you work, the more likely you are to make your wish come true. Before you know it, you'll enjoy the work as much as you enjoy the results. From that point on, the results will take care of themselves.

9. Be brief.

Less is more. The shorter your wish, the greater the emotional impact. A single short sentence is perfect. To keep your wish brief, act as if each word costs you $10,000.

10. Believe in it.

Why would a gardener take the trouble to plant a seed, water it, fertilize it, and tend it—perhaps for weeks—before seeing any return at all on the effort? Because he believes the seed will grow into something worth the effort. Perhaps it will turn into a flower, or a fruit, or a useful vegetable. Whatever the expected result, the expectation must come before the result. The only gardens we bother to tend are the ones we believe will grow.

When you make a wish, you have to believe you will succeed, or else you won't be willing to make the effort. With belief comes action. With action comes results. Without belief there is neither action nor results.

11. Take immediate action.

The final step in making your wish presentable is to send your brain the most powerful message of all: *Act now.* If you don't, you'll fall prey to the Law of Diminishing Intent: the more time that passes before you act, the less likely you will be to take action.

Before you get up from your chair, do something to put your wish into action. Make a phone call, create a plan, read a useful article in a newspaper or magazine, write a letter. Do something to get the ball rolling. *Do anything.* The important thing is to take some kind of action right now, before you lose the moment, and with it your chance to make your wish come true.

Make Your Wish Presentable

If you haven't already been doing so as we've gone along, take the time now to go back and make your wish presentable. Take it through each of the eleven steps. Write it. Make it specific. Make it measurable. Make it all the things it needs to be to come true. Then take immediate action to start you on your way.

If you've come this far and still don't know what to wish for, then make this your first wish: *Wish to know what to wish for.* Make it an official wish. Make it presentable. Take immediate action. Do this now, and you will be launched into a lifetime of making your wishes come true.

5 *Plan*

You know what to wish for. You have committed yourself to pay the price. You have made your wish presentable. Now you need to create a L.A.M.P. Plan to put the L.A.M.P. Process in motion.

A L.A.M.P. Plan is a simple plan of action in which you break your wish into steps so compellingly small that you can't wait to get started on the first one, then the next, and then the one after that, until before you know it you have made your wish come true.

Your L.A.M.P. Plan is a bridge from thinking to doing. It translates your wish from an idea into the actions necessary to turn that idea into reality.

A good plan motivates you to complete even the most minor details because it drapes each one in the larger purpose. When you work any step of the plan, you feel like you're working the whole plan so every step is worth your best effort.

But the magic of your plan is not in the details, it's in the freedom those details give you. Freedom from the distraction of worrying about what to do next. Freedom to focus all your energy and attention on the single step at hand, knowing that every step you complete takes you that much closer to where you want to go. Freedom to try, because you know you'll succeed. A good plan sets your mind at ease and your body in motion. It removes confusion, uncertainty, and doubt so you can concentrate on getting the job done.

Brainstorming a plan

When I create a plan, I start with my objective in mind and then brainstorm how to get there from here. At the top of a piece of paper, I write this question: *What steps do I need to take to* _____ ? Then I simply fill in the blank, ask myself the question, and write my answers.

Let's make up an example. Suppose your wish is to become Director of Finance for Acme Emporium. At the top of a piece of paper you write this question: *What steps do I need to take to become director of finance at Acme Emporium?* Ask yourself this question and write your answers. They might look like this:

1. Call my friends to see if any of them have contacts at Acme Emporium.
2. Identify the specific person I should approach at Acme Emporium.

3. Line up the references most likely to get me this job.
4. Update my résumé.
5. Research Acme Emporium.

Once you have listed as many steps as you can think of, arrange them in the order in which it makes the most sense to execute them:

1. Research Acme Emporium.
2. Call my friends to see if any of them have contacts at Acme Emporium.
3. Identify the specific person I should approach at Acme Emporium.
4. Update my résumé.
5. Line up references most likely to get me this job.

Then you break the larger steps into smaller steps. For example, Step 4 might look like this:

Step 4: Update my résumé.

1. Read a book about writing résumés.
2. Attend a seminar about writing résumés.
3. Ask a friend for advice.
4. Write the first draft.
5. Run the first draft by some friends.
6. Complete my résumé.
7. Make as many copies as I need.

Some of these steps, in turn, might be broken into even smaller steps, and those into smaller steps still. The idea is to keep breaking down major steps until you create steps so small that they appear inviting to you. You want to feel confident that you can go from one step to the next without undue hardship. No step should be so intimidating that you can't face it—or else when you do reach it the whole process will grind to a halt.

After you've broken down one major step this way, repeat the process for each of the others, until each large step is reduced to a series of manageable tasks. You will then have a list of all the steps necessary to take you from where you are to where you want to go. Once you look at this list and realize how easily you can handle everything on it, you will begin to understand how simple it is to make your wish come true. It's like building a ladder and leaning it against a towering tree. When you're done you can stand back, admire your handiwork, and say with conviction, "Now I *know* I can climb it."

Deadlines

You don't have a plan until you have a deadline. The purpose of a deadline is to make you feel a sense of urgency. It lets you know how serious you are about making your wish come true. It switches on the light at the end of the tunnel, so you quicken your pace to reach it.

Set reasonable deadlines. If you want to get a new job, give yourself at least six months, not six weeks. If you want to double your sales, give yourself a year, not a month. If you want to achieve financial independence and you're starting from scratch, give yourself a decade, not a year. A deadline is designed to make you focus, not to make you panic.

When I began *The Magic Lamp,* I set a deadline of seven months to complete it. Seven months later I was delighted with my progress, but I was barely half done. I thought I had let myself down until I realized that my only crime was to underestimate how long it would take me to write the kind of book I wanted to write. Instead of beating myself up, I simply reset my deadline for twelve months rather than seven. In the end the book took fifteen months, more than twice as long as I had originally planned. But I finished it.

The advantage of setting a deadline is that you fix your wish in time, not just in your mind. You begin to plan your life around it, the same way you plan around any other important event. Your wish becomes real, like an appointment, or a holiday, or a business trip you've scheduled for next month. The more real your wish becomes, the more convinced you become that you can make your wish come true.

One frosty afternoon during the winter before I completed *The Magic Lamp,* I remember thinking ahead to the vacation my family and I were planning to spend at the beach the coming summer. I was reviewing where I would be with my various projects by the time we left for vacation when an interesting thought struck me: *The Magic Lamp* would be finished. By then I would be working with my publisher to schedule book signings, publicity interviews, speaking engagements. And I would be halfway through my next book. These events seemed as real to me as if they were already memories.

Except that I didn't have a publisher. I hadn't scheduled any book signings, publicity interviews, or speaking engagements. I hadn't even finished my book. But I had finished my plan. I had set deadlines. The instant I began to schedule around those deadlines, my wish became as real to me as if I had already completed it. In that moment, I knew for certain that I would complete it, just as surely as I knew that I would be lounging on the beach come August.

Once you fix your wish in time, it will feel like the most natural thing in the world to complete it in time. That's the power of a deadline.

Milestones

Milestones are intermediate targets designed to keep you on track toward your main deadline. They help you make continual progress over time, so you don't have to accomplish everything at the last moment.

For example, suppose in November you decide to lose thirty pounds by the time you leave for vacation the following July. To help you meet your deadline, you might set a milestone of losing a pound every week. If you meet each weekly milestone, then by July you will have lost all thirty pounds. If you miss a milestone or two, you still have time to take corrective action—before it's too late.

Scheduling

Once you've listed the steps you need to take to make your wish come true, and you've also set milestones to keep you on track toward your deadline, you need to transfer both the steps and the milestones to your daily schedule. Scheduling bridges the gap between planning and doing. It's the difference between a good intention and an appointment. Instead of saying to an old friend, "Let's have lunch sometime," scheduling lets you say, "Let's have lunch next Tuesday at one P.M."

If you've ever used a pocket scheduler, you already know how to schedule the steps and the milestones of your L.A.M.P. Plan. Simply enter each step in your scheduler the same way you would enter a meeting, or a lunch date, or an appointment with your doctor. You don't have to schedule the entire plan all at once, just the next week or two. Then if a step takes longer than expected, or your schedule is disrupted in some other way, you won't have as much to reschedule.

When you schedule a step on your calendar, you are making an appointment with yourself. Keep it. Treat it like an appointment with the most important person in the world. It is.

Take yourself seriously. If you don't, who will? Take yourself as seriously as you want the rest of the world to take you. After all, why should anyone else treat you better than you treat yourself? If you want other people to keep their appointments with you, keep your appointments with yourself. If you want other people to be there when you need them, be there for yourself.

The Limiting Factor

The *limiting factor* is the bottleneck that can affect how rapidly you make your wish come true. For a L.A.M.P. Plan to be successful, it must be designed to get past this limiting factor.

Consider these examples: Bill is a middle-aged stockbroker whose wish is to get back into shape by exercising at six each morning before he heads to the office. But Bill hates to drag himself out of bed that early, so every morning he invents a new excuse to sleep late, and every morning he skips his workout. Sleeping late is the limiting factor in his plan. If he's ever going to shape up, he first has to get up.

Polly is a computer salesperson who plans to double her sales in the next year, but she is terrified of cold calling for prospects. Fear is her limiting factor. She will have to deal with this fear before she can increase her cold calling enough to double her sales.

Manuel is an unhappy accountant who desperately wants to find a new job, but he can't find the time to look for one. Time management is his limiting factor. He has to learn how to fit job hunting into his already overloaded schedule or he will be stuck in his current job until he retires—or gets fired.

The distinguishing characteristic of a limiting factor is that once you overcome it, everything else falls into place. If Bill develops the habit of bouncing out of bed at six each morning, he will soon be able to work himself into shape. If Polly learns to enjoy cold calling instead of fearing it, her sales will shoot off the chart. If Manuel learns how to manage his time, he will soon find all the time he needs to look for a new job.

Now consider your wish. What is it that most limits your progress? What factor, once changed, will make everything else fall into place? It might be a habit you need to change, as it was with Bill; or a skill you need to acquire, as it was with Manuel; or it might be your way of looking at the world, as it was with

Polly. Once you have pinpointed the limiting factor in your wish, design your L.A.M.P. Plan to overcome it.

When I decided to change careers and become a writer after twenty years in the world of business, I found myself facing a classic limiting factor: I didn't want to write. I thought about writing. I read books about it. I dreamed about being a world-famous author. But the writing itself was a dreadful chore.

Rather than force myself to do something I didn't want to do, I focused my L.A.M.P. Plan on learning how to enjoy the process of writing. When I accomplished that, everything else fell into place.

You will discover the same thing. When you identify the limiting factor for your wish and gear your L.A.M.P. Plan to overcome it, the rest of your wish will fall into place.

Schedule Progress Reports

Once you've listed the steps of your L.A.M.P. Plan and scheduled them on your calendar or daily planner, you need to schedule regular progress reports to see how you're coming along.

A progress report is like looking out the window while you're riding a train. By observing what you're passing, you can tell whether or not the train is going in the right direction. But if you aren't paying attention, you can come to the end of the line and find yourself in the wrong city.

To schedule progress reports, estimate how long it will take you to complete your wish and divide that time into regular intervals. If your wish will take a year, make a progress report for yourself every month. If your wish will take a month, make a progress report every week. Include these reports in your L.A.M.P. Plan. Then schedule them in your calendar, the same way you schedule the other steps of your plan.

When the time comes to make a progress report, write your answers to these questions:

1. Have I met the milestones I planned to meet since my last progress report?
2. Do I need to change my plan to reach my milestones?
3. Do I need to change my milestones?

Circumstances change constantly. Your plan may need to change with them. If you find that you need to make changes, make them. If you need to revise your plan, revise it. That's what a progress report is all about.

End Your Plan with Your Next Wish

The human mind is a problem-solving tool. If you don't give it a problem to solve, it will create one. If you don't give it work to do, it will make work. Or it may prolong what it's currently working on—it may slow down the progress on your wish—just to keep itself occupied.

You can avoid this by having another wish queued up and ready to go. I don't mean you have to jump from one wish right into another. Go ahead and celebrate when you complete a wish. Take a vacation, recharge your batteries. But know what comes next. Know that when it's time to get back to work, you have meaningful work to get back to. No L.A.M.P. Plan is complete until you've included that final step: your next wish.

You are already a master planner, whether you know it or not.

Some people say they don't believe in planning because it takes the spontaneity out of life. I never argue with them, I just change the subject. I ask them where they are going on their next vacation. They light up like kids on Christmas morning. They tell me where they're going, when they'll leave, how long they'll be gone, what they intend to do, what it's going to cost, when they'll return. There's a name for this kind of information—it's called a plan.

Plans work. You've been proving that your whole life. Have you ever taken a vacation and found yourself a thousand miles from where you intended to go? Of course not. Have you ever made it halfway to your destination, then given up and come home? Never happens. When you're on vacation, you know where you want to go, how to get there, when you'll leave, how long you'll stay, when you'll come home—and you're determined to complete the journey.

What if your life worked the same way? It will, if you plan your wishes the way you plan your vacations. In fact, if you take your wishes as seriously as you take your vacations, you just might turn your entire life into a vacation.

L.A.M.P. Process Step 2:

Act

6 *Inertia*

A wish is a self-fulfilled prophecy.
ALAN ELLIS

A plan gives your wish form; action gives it life. Step 1 in the L.A.M.P. Process is to lock on to your wish and plan to make it come true. Step 2 is to take the action called for in your plan.

When you act, you set causes in motion. When you set causes in motion, you are rewarded with effects. When you take action, you make a giant leap from *thinking* your wish to *living* your wish. You change yourself from a dreamer to a doer. To make that leap, you need to overcome one of the greatest forces in nature: inertia.

When I was in college, I decided that I wanted to become a writer. I got out of college and I got a job as a salesman. For years I helped to raise my family, cut the lawn, took out the trash, hung the Christmas lights—I did everything I was supposed to do, except write. As I neared forty, I realized that I was going to have to call my bluff—start writing or give up my dream of being a writer. I decided to stick with my dream, but that still left me with the same problem: How was I going to get myself to write?

Then I remembered something I learned in high school physics: the law of inertia. A body in motion tends to remain in motion; a body at rest tends to remain at rest. I began to wonder if inertia applied to human behavior the way it applied to the behavior of comets streaking past the sun. What if my problem was simply inertia? What if all I had to do was to turn myself from a body at rest to a body in motion?

I decided to find out. I made a commitment to myself to write something every day. It didn't matter how little I wrote: a sentence or two if I wanted, or even a single word if that's all I could muster. But no matter how busy I was, or how distracted, or how tired, I had to write something every day. I promised myself I would try this for thirty days and see what happened.

It worked, and I learned one of the great lessons of my life: Inertia is the single greatest barrier to success. It's also the easiest to overcome. All you have to do is to act. Any action you take, no matter how trivial, will do the trick.

The easier you make it on yourself to act, the easier it is to overcome inertia. For instance, I made it so easy on myself to write that I no longer had any reason not to write. Instead of making a big production out of it, I made it as small a production as I could. I gave myself permission to do nothing more than pound out a few keystrokes on my word processor.

That simple act of typing was all I needed to overcome inertia. With my first keystroke, I turned myself from a body at rest into a body in motion. Once in motion, the most natural thing for me to do was to continue in motion and keep writing. So I did. I would sit to write a single sentence and stand having completed an entire page.

You can overcome your own inertia the same way. Think small. Instead of trying to complete your wish in a single day, focus on a single step, the smallest step you can think of. The moment you take action—any action—you will conquer inertia. You will become a body in motion and will tend to stay in motion. The most natural thing in the world will be for you to take the next step, and then the next, until you've completed your wish.

This simple but profound principle allowed me to breathe new life not only into my writing but into my day job as a salesperson. For years I used to dread the dozens of phone calls I had to make every day. I kept putting them off, and they kept piling up, making me dread them even more. Everything changed when I learned the secret of inertia.

I committed myself to make at least one phone call the moment I got to the office every morning. I didn't have to make twenty calls, or ten, or even five. I just had to make one before I did anything else—before I said good morning to my associates, before I stopped by the water cooler, before I went to the bathroom. The act of dialing that first call transformed me from a body at rest to a body in motion. Once I was a body in motion, it felt only natural to make a second call, then a third. Before I knew it, I was on top of my phone calls instead of having my phone calls on top of me.

I cured more than my phone problem. My whole day became more productive. From the moment I arrived at work, I became a body in motion and tended to stay in motion. As you can imagine, a body in motion gets a lot more work done than a body at rest.

The First Action

A journey of a thousand miles begins with a single step. Your L.A.M.P. Plan, no matter how simple or how complex, begins the same way.

The first action you take is the one that overcomes inertia, the one that transforms you from a body at rest to a body in motion. Take that action and you have the momentum you need to carry you to the next action. That's all you have to worry about. You don't need enough momentum to complete your whole plan; all you need is enough to complete your next action. Then that momentum will carry you to the next action, then the next, then the next after that, until you complete your wish.

The secret of that first action is to make it so simple, so unintimidating, that you give yourself no reason to resist it. For instance, if your wish calls for you to become a concert pianist, tell yourself you're just going to practice a few notes. If you want to look for a new job, tell yourself you're just going to update the first line of your résumé. If you want to become a movie star, tell yourself you're just going to watch a movie to see how the pros do it. If you want to run for president of the United States, jot down the first three things you'll do once you're in office.

You can never finish what you never start. The easier you make it on yourself to take the first action, the greater your chances to make it to the last action, the one that completes your plan and makes your wish come true.

Many First Actions

There are many other "first actions" on your journey, as many as there are stops along the way. Whenever you pause in carrying out your wish—for a phone call, for dinner, to go to work at your day job, to take your summer vacation—you'll find yourself once more in the deadening grip of inertia when you try to resume. Your natural tendency, once stopped, will be to remain stopped. You'll have to find a way to get started all over again.

Think of the smallest and easiest thing you can do to get yourself restarted, and then do it. You don't have to begin at the beginning, you can begin at the point of least resistance. It's like climbing a hill. You don't have to start at the bottom, where the grade looks the steepest. You can start in the middle, or near the top. Then it won't seem so difficult to begin.

Once you do begin, you'll turn yourself into a body in motion and momentum will take care of the rest. Then you'll find how much easier it is to make your wishes come true when the law of inertia is working for you instead of against you.

7 Habits

The easiest actions for us to take are the ones we perform out of habit. The easiest way to grant yourself a wish is to make a habit out of the actions you must take to cause that wish to come true.

You can create new habits the same way you created all of your existing habits—through repetition. Every habit you own you formed by doing something over and over again until it became second nature. To form a new habit, all you have to do is to apply the same principle.

Practice

When I was in high school, I must have tried three or four times to teach myself how to play the guitar. I would open my song book to a Bob Dylan tune and try to place my fingers on the strings the way the book showed me. I would struggle with the chords and my sore fingertips for two or three days and then quit. A year later I would be back at it again: same songs, same guitar, same result.

In college, I met a music major who agreed to teach me how to play guitar, on one condition: I had to practice at least twenty minutes a day for thirty days in a row, to get myself into the habit. If I wasn't willing to practice, he wasn't willing to teach. I agreed to his terms, and after thirty days I was playing the guitar.

My teacher taught me an important lesson about the guitar, but he taught me an even more important lesson about life: In thirty days you can turn almost anything into a habit, if you practice it for a few minutes every day.

Suppose you wish to take a walk each morning to work yourself into shape, but you're having trouble giving up your morning routine—your habit—of reading the newspaper. What you need is a new habit to replace the old one. For thirty days, practice walking each morning instead of reading the paper. At first, you may feel uncomfortable because your old habit still has hold of you. But by the second or third week, you'll begin to find it more natural to walk each morning than to read the paper. After a month of this, you'll find that walking has become your new habit.

If you try this and find that the new habit isn't taking hold, it's probably because you skipped a day. That won't work. You can't afford to skip even a single day. If you do, your momentum will drop to zero, and you'll have to start over again. It's like hitting the brakes when you're driving your car up an icy hill. You can try to get moving again from where you stop, but your best bet is to roll back to the bottom and start over. During that first thirty days, if you miss even a day of practice, reset your thirty-day clock to Day One and start from the beginning. The next time around, practice every day. By the thirtieth day, you will have given yourself a new habit.

Internal Practice

When we think of practice, we usually think of what I call *external practice,* the kind you do with your body. But there is a second kind of practice, one that is equally useful when it comes to developing a new habit and is far easier to perform. I call it *internal practice* because you do it with your mind.

You have been conducting your own internal practice sessions since you were a kid. Remember when you had to give a report before the whole class and you rehearsed it over and over again in your head? Or when you wanted to ask someone out and you rehearsed precisely what you were going to say and how you were going to say it? If you were an athlete, you probably pictured yourself winning. If you were in a play, you pictured yourself performing flawlessly in front of an auditorium full of people. If you were in the band, you imagined yourself hitting all the right notes.

All of these are examples of what psychologists call *visualization.* That's just a fancy word for practicing with your mind instead of your body. The latest research into visualization proves that your mind can't tell much of a difference between an activity you visualize and one you actually perform. This suggests that you can benefit nearly as much from practicing with your mind as you can from practicing with your body.

For example, researchers at Ohio State University divided a group of basketball players into three teams. Each team shot some foul shots, and the researchers recorded the scores. Then for the next month, the first team practiced shooting foul shots for half an hour every day. The second team visualized themselves shooting foul shots for half an hour every day but never actually shot any. The third team neither practiced foul shooting nor visualized themselves doing it.

When the month was up, the researchers retested the shooting skills of each team. The third team, the players who neither practiced nor visualized practicing, showed no improvement at all. The first team, the players who actually practiced foul shooting, improved their results by 28 percent. The second team, the players who visualized themselves shooting foul shots but never shot any, improved by 27 percent—virtually the same amount as the first team, without ever touching a basketball.

How can your mind have such a powerful effect over your body? We don't really know the answer; we just know that it does. And you know it, too, from your own experience. Have you ever bolted awake in the middle of a nightmare, dripping with sweat and shaking with fear? It was all in your mind, but try to explain that to your body. Of course, a nightmare is unintentional. Just imagine what you can accomplish when you put your mind to it.

To practice visualization, try this simple exercise. You'll need to be limber enough to do some twisting and turning, so you might want to warm up and stretch a little before you proceed.

(If you have a bad back, skip this exercise and go to the next one). You'll need at least an arm's length of space around you.

> *1. Stand and extend your arms out to your sides, as if you're an airplane ready for takeoff. Point your index fingers. Notice what your right index finger is pointing at. Now twist at the waist as far as you can—keeping your arms extended—and notice what your finger is pointing at when you can't twist any farther. Twist back to center, drop your arms, take a couple of deep breaths, and relax.*

> *2. Close your eyes. In your mind's eye, perform the twisting exercise you just completed, but this time, see yourself twisting farther, past where you stopped before. Remember what your index finger was pointing at when you stopped the first time? This time around, picture what your finger will be pointing at as it twists past that first stopping point.*

> *3. Open your eyes and perform for real what you just pictured in your mind. Chances are, you twisted farther the second time because you pictured yourself doing so. You practiced it in your mind; then your brain interpreted your mental practice as if it were a real experience. When you executed your second twist, you were able to perform with your body what you had already performed with your mind.*

Here's another exercise: Extend your arms straight out in front of you, perfectly level with each other and parallel to the ground. Close your eyes and imagine that someone has just slipped the handle of a pail full of water into your left hand, and you're straining with all your might to support the pail and keep your arm level. Into your right hand, someone slips a string. Tied to the end of the string is a large helium-filled balloon. As the balloon floats upward, it gently pulls your right arm along with it, while your left arm is struggling with the pail of water that seems to grow heavier by the second.

Now open your eyes. Chances are, your arms are no longer level. When your mind painted its pictures—the pail of water in one hand and the balloon in the other—your body had no choice but to respond. That's the power of visualization.

Pre-Memory

The term *visualization* is misleading. Internal practice is far more than seeing the appropriate pictures in your mind. You must also feel the appropriate feelings, hear the appropriate sounds, taste the appropriate tastes, and smell the appropriate smells. You need to experience your practice session in your mind as if you were actually experiencing it with your body. The more realistic you make your mental practice, the more firmly you fix the "experience" in your brain.

Sometimes a mental experience is so powerful that it feels like a memory instead of like something you just dreamed up. I call this kind of intense mental image a *pre-memory*. This is something you "remember" before it happens, because you want to make it happen the way you've "remembered" it. You imagine the pictures, feelings, and sounds of your experience, and the tastes and smells if there are any, as clearly as if they had already happened.

Pre-memories are the most powerful kind of internal practice, rivaling the memories you retain from actual experience. Your mind can tell so little difference between what's real and what you've imagined that you can use pre-memories to create new habits the same way you've used actual experience to create your existing habits. All it takes is repetition.

To use pre-memories to form a new habit, just ask yourself these three questions:

1. What would I see through my own eyes if I were actually practicing my new habit?
2. What would I hear?
3. How would I feel?

Suppose you want to create a new habit of reading in the evening when you get home from work, to replace your old habit of collapsing on the couch and staring at the TV. First, picture your TV. Then picture your hand reaching out to turn it off. In your mind's ear, listen to the "click" of the on-off switch, and hear the dialogue die in mid-sentence, leaving only silence.

Now picture your hand picking up a good book. Picture your home as you move through it to find a seat in your favorite chair or sofa. How would the room look around you? How would you feel as you settled into a comfortable position in your chair?

Picture your hands opening the book. How would the pages look? How would they feel? What sound would they make? To deepen your experience, ask yourself this question:

How would I feel if I really were enjoying this new habit?

Internal practice is an effective substitute for external practice, but the best way to create a new habit is to use both. Practice your new habit externally at least once a day. Then practice it internally at least once a day. If you do both, you will learn your new habit more quickly than you ever thought possible.

Affirmations

There is a second kind of internal practice that appears so simple it's hard to believe it really works, but it does. And you've been practicing it since you were old enough to speak.

Though we hate to admit it, we all talk to ourselves. More important, we all listen. Psychologists call this *affirmation*. What they mean is this: If you tell yourself something often enough, you begin to believe it.

Most of us are pretty good at affirming our shortcomings. We knock over an iced tea at a lawn party and say, "I'm so clumsy!" We forget to bring our briefcase to work and say, "I'd forget my own head if it weren't screwed on!" We make a mistake quoting a price to a customer and say, "I'm so lousy at math I can't even balance my own checkbook!"

But we can affirm our strengths, too. We can even affirm strengths we don't yet have, as a way of developing them into habits.

For instance, if you would like to become the kind of person who bounces out of bed every morning at six, you can tell yourself: *I love to rise each morning at six, refreshed and invigorated for the entire day.* If you're a salesperson and you want to learn to love prospecting for new business, you can tell yourself: *I love to prospect for new customers.* If you want to develop the habit of better time management, you can tell yourself: *I love to plan my work and work my plan.*

I've used affirmations to create all sorts of useful habits. For example, I used to hate to solve problems. Whenever I encountered a problem, my habit was to duck it and hope it would go away. After forty years of hiding my head in the sand, I realized that I would never get what I wanted from life until I learned how to solve the problems that stood in my way. It wasn't enough for me just to face problems; I wanted to learn how to enjoy solving them, so I made the following contract with myself:

> *For thirty days, at least ten times a day, I agree to tell myself:* I love to solve problems. *I agree to say it with the kind of heartfelt conviction that will leave no room for doubt. At the end of thirty days, if I still hate to solve problems, I will allow myself to cling to that habit for the rest of my life.*

Then I went to work. The first couple of days I felt resistance. Every time I repeated my affirmation, an angry little voice in my mind would say, "Who are you trying to kid with this affirmation crap? You hate to solve problems!" I couldn't disagree with that (and I didn't want to lie to myself) so I pretended I was an actor, playing the part of a character who loved to solve problems. Before I knew it, the resistance disappeared.

Within a week, I began to enjoy repeating my affirmation. Within two weeks, I began to look forward to saying it. It made me feel good, as if I were lifting a massive load from my shoulders every time I said it. Often I would repeat my affirmation more than ten times, just for the fun of it. I even began to laugh when I said it because saying it made me feel so good. I knew that if I could learn how to love solving problems, then I could accomplish anything. No wonder I felt giddy at the prospect!

By the end of the thirty days, I found myself looking for problems to solve. Whenever I encountered one, I would hear myself say: *I love to solve problems!* Then I would plunge right in and solve it. My affirmation had come true, and that allowed me to make a quantum leap forward in my life.

The first step in creating an affirmation is to make certain it supports your values. If you feel it's unethical or undesirable, then it won't work (and you wouldn't want it to). The next step is to follow similar guidelines to those you used when you created a presentable wish. Be specific. Affirm what you want instead of what you don't want. Use the present tense. Give it intense emotional impact.

That last point is the one that counts the most. The real power of an affirmation comes from how deeply you feel it, not from how many times you say it. You want emotional content, not repetition for the sake of repetition. But how can you feel emotion about something you don't really believe?

Don't worry about whether you believe an affirmation, worry about whether you *want* to believe it. If you want to believe it— if you intensely want to believe it—and you repeat it with that same intensity, then you will soon come to believe it, the same way you've come to believe so much negative garbage about yourself. If you're going to pump yourself full of propaganda anyway, why not choose propaganda that serves a useful purpose?

Just make certain that your affirmations contain emotional words like *love* and *joy*, and let yourself feel those words when you say them. Emotion is the magic ingredient that will turn your affirmations into reality.

As the days pass, you'll find it easier to move your behavior into line with your affirmation. The trick is not to force yourself, but to listen to yourself. For example, if your affirmation is *I prefer to eat healthy food*, that doesn't mean you have to give up junk food on the spot. Listen to your affirmation. Feel it. Then gradually change your behavior when it feels right. Before you know it, you'll find yourself substituting an apple for a candy bar and pasta for fried chicken. Within thirty days, you'll start to think differently about what you eat, so it will seem only natural to eat differently as well.

Positive Thinking

Some people think that affirmations are the same as positive thinking and they think that positive thinking is trying to fool yourself into feeling what you don't actually feel. When it doesn't work, when they try to think positive but they still feel lousy, they get frustrated and say that positive thinking doesn't work, that it's all a come on, a lie.

But they miss the point. Positive thinking is not a matter of trying to fool yourself, it's a matter of directing your thoughts to the positive. Take these thoughts, for example:

> *Is the glass half full or half empty?*
> *Isn't the darkest hour just before dawn?*

Today is the first day of the rest of your life.
Are you part of the problem or part of the solution?

These are among the great clichés of positive thinking. They have become objects of ridicule by cynics who can't shake their own negative way of looking at the world. But that belies the power these thoughts have to redirect your thinking. Positive thinking isn't about lying to yourself, it's about acknowledging that there is both a positive and a negative side to every circumstance, and we have the power to dwell on one or the other. We can choose the cloud or the silver lining.

Affirmations, on the other hand, are a way to practice a new way of thinking. Just as you had to practice when you were learning how to ride a bicycle because riding a bicycle was strange and uncomfortable at first, you have to practice new ways of thinking because they may feel strange and uncomfortable at first. Affirmations allow you to conduct such practice and develop new habits of thinking.

Schedule Your Practice

Schedule the date and time for your practice sessions, the same way you schedule other important appointments. Then honor your schedule. If you have trouble keeping appointments with yourself, then that's the first habit you need to change. Learn to treat an appointment with yourself the same way you would treat an appointment with the president of the United States. Even if you didn't vote for him, you probably wouldn't keep him waiting.

Thirty-Day Plan

You can turn almost anything into a habit if you implement what I call a *Thirty-Day Plan*. All you have to do is to decide what new habit you want to acquire and then agree to practice that habit every day for just thirty days. If in thirty days you don't like the results, quit. That's all there is to it.

Make sure you schedule each day's practice and then honor your schedule. Don't let yourself skip days because of weekends, or holidays, or illness, or because you had to go out of town. Don't accept any excuses for missing even a single day. If you do miss a day, start over.

The beauty of a Thirty-Day Plan is that it minimizes your natural resistance to change. You aren't asking yourself to give up anything; you're just asking yourself to try something new for a while. You can stand almost anything for a few days. After thirty days, if you don't like your new habit, you're free to go back to the old one. But the chances are that by then your new habit will feel more comfortable than the one it has replaced.

8 Comfort Zone

Have you ever wondered why most New Year's resolutions rarely last beyond New Year's Day? Have you ever wondered why habits are so hard to break? Have you ever wondered why even the best intentions of one moment are forgotten in the rush of the next?

At home, you probably set your thermostat to turn on the air conditioning if the temperature gets too high, say 78 degrees, or to turn on the heater if the temperature falls too low, say 68 degrees. These settings create what is known in the heating-and-cooling business as a *comfort zone*. Whenever the temperature moves beyond the zone, the thermostat automatically makes the adjustments necessary to bring it back within the zone.

The human mind works much the same way. Each of us has our own internal "comfort settings" by which we tend to operate, like the upper and lower settings of a thermostat. We regulate our behavior by these settings, the way a thermostat regulates the temperature of a room. Whenever our life falls too far below our settings or rises too far above them, our mental thermostat kicks in to bring us back within our comfort zone.

When we make a New Year's resolution or try to change an old habit, we move ourselves beyond our comfort zone. But not for long. Our mental thermostat will soon do whatever it needs to do to bring us back to where we belong. Before we know it, our good intentions are forgotten, and we're back in the same old rut. No wonder it seems so hard to change.

A wish, like a New Year's resolution, takes you beyond your comfort zone. If you want to make certain a wish comes true, you will have to adjust your comfort zone to accommodate that wish. If you don't, sooner or later you will find yourself giving up your wish and returning to your old familiar ways.

Adjusting Your Comfort Zone

To adjust your comfort zone, you have only to change the settings in your mind, much the way you would change the settings of a thermostat to adjust the comfort zone of a room. Once you change yourself on the inside, the outside will soon catch up. Change your idea of how you should live, and you will soon change how you do live. That's the way human beings operate.

Your comfort zone is determined by your habits, specifically, by the mental movies you show yourself through force of habit. To change your comfort zone, simply change your movies. Your mind will then regulate your actions according to the new settings, the way it used to regulate your actions according to the old settings.

To change your movies, think of your mind as your own private movie theater. You are the projectionist. You control the sound, the brightness, the color, even the speed at which you roll the film. You can show whatever movies you choose for as long as you choose. You can run the same movies over and over, or just your favorite scenes. If you don't like a movie you're showing, you can stop it mid-scene and show something else.

Because your movies are habits, you can change them the same way you can change any other habits—with practice. Practice a new movie for thirty days, without missing a day, and you will begin to play it automatically, the same way you used to play the old one. Keep practicing until your new movie feels as natural as the old one.

For example, suppose you decide to replace your old habit of sleeping late with a new habit of rising at 6 A.M., so you have some free time to work on your wish before you head to the office. The problem is, you hate to get out of bed that early. Just thinking about your alarm going off at 6 A.M. fills you with dread. You can't even imagine yourself getting up.

That's because you're running the wrong movie. So run a different one. Show a movie in which you can't wait to bounce out of bed at six, energized for the whole day. Fill yourself with expectation instead of dread. Feel the exhilaration of having the world by the tail because you've become the master of your own sleeping habits.

Watch your new movie as if you were seeing it through your own eyes, rather than as a spectator. Play the movie over and over—at least five times a day—and make doubly sure you roll it whenever you find yourself thinking about how early you have to get up the next morning.

The idea is to turn your new movie into a pre-memory, so you can roll it as easily as you used to roll the old movie. Imagine yourself getting up at 6 A.M. as if you already do it. Live it in your mind. Feel your eyes popping open at six, without an alarm. Notice how wonderful it feels to bounce out of bed full of energy, ready to meet your day. Hear yourself say how great it makes you feel. Keep practicing your new movie until it feels as natural as the old movie. Keep practicing it until it becomes the movie you automatically launch each morning when it's time to get up.

Meanwhile, practice an affirmation. If you're the kind of person who likes to sleep late, the chances are you've been telling yourself that for years. So tell yourself something different. Instead of saying, "I love to sleep late," tell yourself *I love to rise at six each morning, refreshed and invigorated for the entire day.* Say it with genuine emotion, not because it's true, but because you want it to become true. Repeat it with intense emotion ten times a day for thirty days. As you do, you'll find it easier and easier to run your new movie. The easier it gets to run your new movie, the easier it gets to jump out of bed.

When you turn this new movie into a habit, you will have successfully adjusted the settings of your comfort zone. At that point, rising at 6 A.M. will seem like the most natural thing in the world to do, more natural than sleeping late.

When you change your comfort zone, you change your life. In junior high school, I hated to run any farther than from the TV to the refrigerator. I was also dreadfully overweight. One summer I decided to get into shape by jogging a mile each day around a nearby track. Each afternoon, dripping sweat as I baked under the sun, I would begin my first lap around that steamy cinder track, wondering every step of the way if I could make it a whole mile. It was horrible. It was torture. It was worse than being fat. I fought myself every step, every day, until finally I gave up.

A couple of years later, in high school, I joined the cross-country team. Back on that same cinder track where I used to hate to jog a mile, under that same fiery sun, the cross-country team jogged two miles every day—*just to warm up*. And I jogged with them.

Somewhere along the line, without realizing it, I had changed the movie I was showing in my mind. I used to picture running as agony, but by the time I joined the cross-country team I had learned to picture running as fun. Once I changed the movie in my mind, my body took the change for granted. By changing the settings of my comfort zone, I changed what had been torture into nothing more than a warm-up.

When you learn how to change your comfort zone to accommodate your wishes, you'll find it the most natural thing in the world to make those wishes come true.

Discomfort

The thing to keep in mind about making any kind of change, whether it's changing a habit or changing your comfort zone, is that the process of change itself is uncomfortable. When you make a change, the chances are that at first you're going to feel some mild discomfort. That's not a symptom that something is wrong; it's a symptom that something is right. The discomfort is telling you that you're going beyond what you're accustomed to. You're attempting something that you aren't yet comfortable with because you want to become comfortable with it. You're stretching the old you in a new direction that will eventually produce a new and better you.

That's called growth. And growth is what life is all about. Somebody once said that if you aren't growing, you're dying. In a strictly physical sense, that's true. Once our cells stop growing, our body starts to die. But it's also true mentally. When it comes to our emotions, our capacities, and our talents, if we aren't growing them, then we're losing them. If we aren't expanding our horizons, then we're allowing them to close in on us. If we aren't demanding more from our lives and from ourselves, then we're accepting less.

Learn to expect the discomfort of change and to embrace it as proof that you're still alive, still vigorous, still growing. The moment you stop changing, you stop growing. The moment you stop growing, you stop living.

Cultivate change; accept discomfort; insist on growth. When you do, your comfort zone will expand to make your wishes come true.

9 *Time*

You have your wish, you have your plan, and you're taking the action necessary to make your wish come true. Now all you have to do is to give it time.

There are two kinds of time. The first kind is measured by the number of hours you are willing to devote to a task during a single day. I call this *vertical time*. The second kind is measured by the number of days you are willing to devote to a task in order to complete it. I call this *horizontal time*. The maximum *vertical time* at our command is 24 hours because that's all the time there is in a day. The maximum *horizontal time* at our command is an entire lifetime. Which kind of time do you think is more powerful?

All hours are not created equal. If a crack appeared in a dam behind your house and it was going to take 24 hours to fix it, would you work on it an hour a day for 24 days? Of course not. You would work on it around the clock until you fixed the problem because you wouldn't want the dam to burst and wash your house away. But what if you wanted to tend a garden in front of that same house? Would you work on it 24 hours a day? Of course not. You would work on it an hour a day for 24 days. And both you and the garden would be better off because of it.

Some tasks require vertical time. Others require horizontal time. Choosing the right kind of time for the job is half the battle. Most people approach their wishes as if they are repairing a dam that is about to break. But most wishes are more like tending a garden than they are like fixing a dam. Most of what you want to accomplish in life you can accomplish better, and with greater enjoyment, if you do it over time, instead of trying to do it all at once.

Unfortunately, the frantic pace of life points us in the opposite direction. Haste has become an end in itself. We would rather work feverishly on a project for a few days than work steadily for a few weeks. We would rather get rich quickly than get rich slowly. And that's where we miss the boat.

It's a lot harder to get rich quickly than it is to get rich slowly. It's a lot harder to accomplish anything of value in a few days than it is to accomplish the same thing in a few months. When you try to cram too much into a single day, or a few days, time is working against you. But when you spread your efforts over time, time is on your side.

Devote even a few minutes a day to a project, and with enough days, you can accomplish almost anything. If you work on your wish over time, over time your wish will come true.

Given enough horizontal time, you can learn to play a musical instrument, master a foreign language, read the collected works of William Shakespeare, dig yourself a swimming pool, earn a college degree, build an addition on your house, learn a trade, write a book, land a new job, start a company, or all of the above. It might take you a year, or it might take you twenty years—so what?

Don't get hung up on how long it will take; that's just another way to derail your dreams. Think of the middle-aged woman who wanted to go to law school but was afraid she was too old. "It will take me three years to finish," she explained to a friend, "and by then I'll be fifty-seven." Her friend asked, "How old will you be in three years if you don't go to law school?"

Who cares how old you are? Who cares how long your L.A.M.P. Plan will take? Of this one thing in life you can be certain: The time will pass anyway; why not put it to good use?

The Gift of Hindsight

As I've already mentioned, when I was a senior in college I decided that I was going to become a writer. But after I graduated, years passed—twelve years to be exact—and I was no closer to becoming a writer than I was the day I left school. Then one morning while I was sitting at my desk hard at work, I had one of those life-changing revelations that comes out of nowhere and takes a baseball bat to the side of your head:

> *If you had decided to write a paragraph a day twelve years ago, by now you would have completed half a dozen books.*

I was stunned. In one traumatic moment I realized just how much time I had wasted, and just how easily I could have prevented that waste. A paragraph a day would have taken me fifteen or twenty minutes, about as much time as I spent shaving and showering each morning. If I had set aside just that much time every day to write, I would have had a whole briefcase full of books with my name on them. But those books didn't exist, because I hadn't taken the time to write them.

For somebody who wanted very much to be a writer, this was beyond painful. I felt as if I were standing on the bank of a river watching a dozen years of my life float by without me. All because I hadn't found the time to write just a single paragraph each day. What kind of an idiot had I been?

Before I could answer that, a new thought presented itself, shining like a sunbeam that has punched its way through a thundercloud:

> *You're missing the point—this is a wake-up call, not Judgment Day.*

Then I finally got it. I finally understood what the world was trying to teach me. The point of life is not to grieve over a wasted past, but to make certain that you don't waste the future. I had been shown my failure so that I could learn from it and turn it into success. All I had to do was to write a paragraph a day *from that point on,* and my dream of being a writer would come true.

Hallelujah! I felt as if I had been handed one of the secrets of the universe. I was delighted, elated, and overjoyed.

I was also terrified.

What if I couldn't change? What if I couldn't muster even the minimal effort necessary to write a paragraph a day? I had never been able to do it before; what made me I think I could do it now?

As if on cue, my thoughts leaped twelve years into the future. There I could see myself wringing my hands in frustration because I still hadn't written a thing. I was miserable, a wretched failure, accused and tormented by regret. I knew I would remain a failure until my dying day. I knew I would live without joy, without reward, without happiness, without . . .

That did it. I'd had enough. I was a changed man. I was bound and determined that I would never let that kind of future take place. Like Scrooge on Christmas morning, I had seen the Ghost of Things Yet to Come, and he had scared the daylights out of me.

I had been given a second chance, and I would make the most of it. The next twelve years would see a very different me from the twelve years just passed.

We are all wise in hindsight. The secret to making your wishes come true is to turn hindsight into foresight. Use your past to empower your future. Begin today what you regret not having done yesterday, and you will avoid that regret tomorrow.

Ellis's Law

Once I began to write every day, the results astonished me. Even when I managed no more than a sentence or two, over time my sentences formed paragraphs, the paragraphs formed chapters, and the chapters formed books—like magic.

But it wasn't magic. It was a simple principle that lies behind all human accomplishment:

Even ordinary effort over time yields extraordinary results.

I call this Ellis's Law, not because I discovered it, but because it discovered me. It's the heart and soul of how I've made my wishes come true. It's the magic behind my magic lamp.

This is the single most important idea in *The Magic Lamp*, the single most useful piece of advice I can give you to help you make your wishes come true. It is so important that I'm going to say it again:

Even ordinary effort over time yields extraordinary results.

If you act on this one piece of advice—even if you ignore everything else you find in these pages—you will multiply a hundredfold your chances for success because you will enlist in your cause the most irresistible force in the universe: *time.*

We're surrounded by testimony to the power of time. The gentle hills on the horizon were once great mountains; the great mountains were once the ocean floor. That sapling we planted years ago grows too slowly for us to notice, yet now it shades the whole house. A bricklayer places a single brick at a time, yet before we know it, he builds a skyscraper. A small drip from a faucet soon fills a bathtub, and given enough time the drip would fill an ocean. We buy a CD of our favorite music, add another and then another over the years, and before we know it our music collection is worth more than our car. We munch an extra cookie after dinner once or twice a week, and the next time we step on the scale, we've gained twenty pounds. Whatever we do over time, we magnify by the time over which we do it. We collect compound interest on everything we do, when we do it long enough.

When I refer to "ordinary effort," I don't mean to suggest that your efforts should be ordinary. Extraordinary effort over time produces even better results. But most of us already know this. We've heard the stories of successful people who have worked extraordinarily hard and produced spectacular results. What most of us miss is the notion that *any* effort can produce results—astonishing results—if we give it enough time.

We don't have to work sixteen-hour days to write a book; we can work twenty minutes a day over the next few years. We don't have to earn a million dollars in the next year to become a millionaire; we can save a few dollars a week for twenty years and accomplish the same thing. We don't have to lose fifty pounds during the next month to look good; we can lose a pound a week for the next fifty weeks and come out looking just as thin. You don't have to get that college degree all at once (or build that rec room, or learn that new language, or earn that promotion); you can work on it an hour or two a day for as long as it takes.

Find the Time to Succeed

Success takes time, even if it's just a few minutes a day. You may feel you don't have a lot of time. You may feel rushed, perhaps even crushed by the pace of life. You may be asking yourself: How will I ever find the time to work a wish into a schedule like mine?

That's the wrong question to ask. Instead of starting with your schedule and trying to work in your wish, start with your wish and then try to work in the rest of the things on your schedule. If you're going to shortchange something, shortchange the things that are at the bottom of your list of priorities, not the things at the top. Make this one change in how you spend your day— work on what is most important to you *before* you take care of everything else—and you'll find that your schedule begins to take on the shape of a life, instead of your life taking on the shape of a schedule.

That still leaves the question: Where will you find the time to get it all done? Many of us don't have to look far. A recent study by Nielsen Media Research found that 98 percent of the homes in the United States have television sets. The average man watches 3 hours and 44 minutes of television every day. The average woman watches 4 hours and 25 minutes. The average teenager watches an average of 2 hours and 43 minutes a day. If you watch as much TV as the average American—even if you watch only half as much—you can find all the time you need to make your wish come true just by turning a portion of your TV time into wish time. Whether it's an hour a day, or half an hour a day, or even fifteen minutes a day, every minute helps. Every minute you spend in front of your wish instead of in front of your TV will move you one minute closer to making your wish come true.

Am I suggesting that you have to give up television to make your wish come true? Of course not. You probably don't watch as much TV as the average American anyway, or you wouldn't have found the time to read this book. Watch as much TV as you like. Just keep this in mind: Of the TV you do watch, there isn't a moment that gets you closer to making your wish come true. If you want more out of life than you're getting now, you have to transform time that isn't giving you what you want into time that is giving you what you want.

It's not a matter of giving up TV or giving up anything else you like to do. It's just a matter of doing what is most important to you *first*. For example, suppose one evening you were about to settle down in front of your favorite TV program when a little voice asked, "Which is more important to you—to make your wish come true or to watch this show?" Which would you choose? Choose your wish, and you're on your way to making that wish come true. Choose your TV program, and you're on your way to watching it. Your wish will just have to wait until it becomes more important than your show. It's as simple as that.

TV time isn't the only time you can use to work on your wish. Do you read the newspaper each morning? It's great to be informed, but is that more important to you than making your wishes come true? Do you read pulp fiction to escape from the rat race? If you invest some of your reading time in making your wishes come true, you might not have as much need to escape.

How much time do you spend each morning getting ready for work? Try cutting it by ten minutes. Then invest those ten minutes in helping to make your wish come true. You would be amazed how much you can accomplish in just ten minutes a day, if you do it every day.

How much time do you spend each day doing chores around the house? Trim a few minutes from each task and use those minutes to work on your wish. You'll still get your chores done, believe it or not, and you'll get your wish done, too.

The Time Tithe

There are two ways to find enough time to work on your wish. The simplest and most direct way is to schedule the time and then stick to your schedule. I schedule time to work on my wish every morning, first thing, because my wish is the most important thing I have to do each day. You might choose to work on your wish at the end of the day, or in the middle. It doesn't matter when you do it; it matters only that you do it, and do it every day.

The second way to make room each day for your wish is to tithe your time. Simply trim by 10 percent the time you spend on each of your daily activities. Then invest that extra time in making your wish come true.

You might think you can't possibly trim any time from your daily activities, but you can. The most curious principle of time management is that the less time we have to do something, the more likely we are to get it done. That's why deadlines work. That's why more Americans file their tax returns a week before they're due than file them a month before they're due. That's why stores on Christmas Eve are so full of people doing last-minute shopping—because it's the last minute they can shop.

The second most curious principle of time management is that the less time we have, the more we tend to get done. We force ourselves to set priorities. We force ourselves to concentrate on the things that are most important to us and ignore the rest. That's why we often accomplish more the day before we leave for vacation than we do the whole week before. The less you have of any precious resource, the more you tend to stretch it to make do.

Start your time tithe with your daily routine. For example, you don't have to give up the morning paper; just trim 10 percent from the time you spend reading it. Trim 10 percent from the time you spend taking a shower, getting dressed, commuting to work, and then watching TV when you come home. Trim 10 percent from the time you spend sleeping. Whatever activities you perform each day, give yourself 10 percent less time to perform each one. This will free two-and-a-half hours every day to devote to your wish, more than enough time to make almost any wish come true.

Work

How can you cut 10 percent from the time you spend at work? If normally you work more than eight hours a day, you can probably cut back to eight hours without coming to grief with your employer. This will become easier when the two of you realize that the quality of your work will tend to improve with less overtime because you will be forcing yourself to set priorities and focus your efforts. You will also feel fresher and more energized while you're at work because you'll be spending less time on the job and more time recharging yourself for the next day's work.

But what if you're already working only eight hours a day and your employer refuses to let you trim that by 10 percent? Just give yourself a work wish, something that you would very much like to make happen at work. Treat this work wish like any other wish. Take it through the L.A.M.P. Process. Work on it every day. To find time to work on it, trim 10 percent from the time you spend on each of the other tasks you have to perform during the work day. Ten percent of an eight-hour day is 48 minutes. That's nearly an hour a day you can use to make your work wish come true.

Sleep

Assuming you average eight hours of sleep a night, if you reduce that by 10 percent you can reclaim nearly an hour a day to work on your wish. But is it wise to cut into your sleep?

I can't give you medical advice (consult your doctor before you decide to change your sleeping habits), but I can tell you what happened to me when I changed my sleeping habits.

A while back I read a curious little book about how to sleep less and enjoy it more. (See the Resources section under "Sleep" at the end of this book.) This little book made two points that really hit home. First, it suggested that the amount of sleep we need seems to be more a matter of habit than of physical necessity. The human body does not require eight hours of sleep each night. There are many people—entire cultures, for that matter—who get by with only six or seven hours of sleep a night. The second point the book made is that someone who is sleeping eight hours every night is probably getting more sleep than he or she needs. Too much sleep can make you as groggy as too little.

I was intrigued with the notion that the eight hours of sleep I thought I required each night might be more of a habit than a necessity. I was equally intrigued by the possibility that I might be able to reduce my sleep by an hour every night and thereby create an extra hour every day to make my wish come true. With so much at stake, I decided to use my habit-changing tools (visualization, affirmation, pre-memory, and repetition) to form a new habit of sleeping only seven hours a night instead of eight.

For the first few days I felt groggy, but before long I found that seven hours of sleep per night was all I needed. I had more energy during the day than ever before, and I slept better at night. To top it off, I gave myself an extra hour every day to work on my wish. That was the equivalent of nine extra work weeks every year.

Try the time tithe for a month and see what happens. Trim just 10 percent from the time you spend on each of your daily activities, then rechannel that 10 percent toward making your wishes come true. You will be investing your most precious asset—your time—toward your most important objective— your wish. Elementary as this may sound, it's the most important thing you can do to make your wish come true.

Give Yourself Time

If your wish is going to take awhile, give it awhile. Give it twice awhile. Make sure your L.A.M.P. Plan allows you enough time to make the plan work. Often when people don't complete a wish in the time they've allowed, they give up and feel like failures. But they aren't failures; they just haven't allowed themselves enough time to get the job done. To make a wish come true, sometimes you have to stick by the wish's schedule instead of your own. You have to give it as much time as it requires. A second less won't do.

The surest way to starve yourself of time is to starve yourself of money. I started a business once that I was certain was going to make me rich. I never worked so hard in my life—sixteen hours a day, seven days a week. I didn't have any money coming in, so I used my savings to pay the bills. When I exhausted my savings, I began to borrow on credit cards. When I filled my credit cards I began to borrow from my family. Before I knew it I was a mile deep in debt and not an inch closer to success. When

I couldn't beg or borrow any more money, I closed my business and went to work for someone else.

The business wasn't a bad idea, but the business plan was. It didn't provide enough money to complete the plan. I should have kept my day job and developed my business part-time. Then I would have had all the income I needed to keep the doors open long enough for my business to take hold. A day job would have given me the horizontal time I needed to make the business work.

Years later, I found myself in a similar situation. I wanted to become a writer. But I wasn't about to quit my day job to write. I knew better. I knew it would take months to finish the first book I had in mind. Then it would take months to sell it to a publisher, if I sold it at all. Then it would take a year before the book found its way into bookstores, and several more years before I had written and sold enough books even to begin to pay my bills. The only way I could give myself the horizontal time I needed to succeed as a writer was to write part-time, and keep my day job for as long as it would take me to become a success.

So that's what I did. It took years. It took years longer than I had imagined. But it worked, because this time around I didn't starve my wish. I never ran out of cash, so I never ran out of time. I allowed myself as much time as I needed to make my wish come true, so it came true.

If you find yourself tempted to quit your day job to pursue your wish, go ahead, as long as you have enough money in the bank to keep yourself going for *twice as long as you think it will take.* If you don't have that much money socked away, do yourself and your wish a favor—keep your day job. If you don't have a day job, get one that pays the bills. Don't think of it as giving up on your wish; think of it as funding your wish so you don't have to give up on it. Your day job can give you all the resources you need to work on your wish for as long as it takes to make that wish come true.

Spare-time wishing may not feel like the ideal arrangement. It may not get you where you want to go as fast as you want to get there, but it will get you there faster than going broke. And it really works. As a young man, Albert Einstein worked as a patent clerk. In his spare time, he invented the Theory of Relativity. Anything is possible if you give it enough time.

Take Your Time

Once you have given yourself enough time to make your wish come true, take your time. Don't rush yourself. Relax and get to work, confident that you have all the time you need to make your wish come true.

I feel most stressed and least productive when I rush through a task. But when I allow myself to take my time, I relax and the quality of my work improves. I feel more creative and more energetic, and I get more done.

Better yet, I enjoy what I'm doing. I enjoy almost any task as long as I'm not racing through it to get to the next one. Even chores like washing dishes and mowing the lawn lose their sense of drudgery when I allow myself to take my time.

In taking my time, I give myself permission to enjoy what I'm doing. This works even when I'm facing a deadline. Whenever I find myself focusing more on the deadline than on what I'm doing, I change the deadline to give myself some breathing room. Once I'm free to take my time, I'm free to enjoy my time, and I'm that much more likely to do my best work.

Take your time, and you'll find that you begin to enjoy what you're doing. Enjoy what you're doing, and you'll find that before you know it you will have completed everything necessary to make your wish come true.

10 *Managing Time*

We've taken a look at the two kinds of time, vertical and horizontal. We've seen how to find more time in even the busiest schedule. Now we need to concentrate on how to manage time so effectively that we make our wishes come true.

When it comes right down to it, time management isn't very complicated. In fact, all of time management can be reduced to a single, breathtakingly simple principle:

First things first.

This principle, in turn, translates into two steps:

1. Figure out the most important thing for you to be doing right now.
2. Do it.

Everything else is filler. The principles and the practices that pass for time management these days fall into two categories: either they help you execute these two steps, or they waste your time.

Time management begins when you ask yourself this question: What is the most important thing for me to be doing right now? Once you answer that question, everything else falls into place.

When you ask yourself this question, sometimes an answer springs to mind. But often, perhaps more often than not, the answer is hard to come by. When this happens, the most important thing for you to do is to figure out the most important thing for you to do.

If this sounds like gratuitous advice, think again. How many times have you lost yourself in busywork without ever pausing to determine if that busywork is worth doing? For many of us, this is a constant struggle. We like to be busy. In the absence of knowing what we should be doing, we all too often get lost in whatever there is to do.

The process of deciding what is most important to you is intimately wrapped up in who you are and what you want from life. If you don't have a handle on this information, then that is where you should begin. You already have the perfect tool to assist you in your research: brainstorming. So let's put that tool to good use.

Brainstorm each of the five questions below, one at a time. Use a separate sheet of paper for each one so you're starting fresh each time. (Before you begin, you might want to review the five steps of the brainstorming process, in chapter 1.)

1. What kind of person am I?
2. What kind of person do I want to become?

3. What values are important to me? (Once you have a list of your values, make sure you do a bubble sort to prioritize them.)
4. What do I want to accomplish during my lifetime?
5. What do I want from life?

Once you have brainstormed each of these questions, you will have the basic information you need to decide what is important for you to be doing, and what is not. You will know how each prospective task fits into the larger picture of who you are and what you want. In short, you will know where to begin.

Important vs. Urgent

Part of knowing where to begin is understanding the difference between what is important and what is urgent. An important task is one that moves your life in the direction you want to go. An urgent task is one that is supposed to be performed at once, whether it moves your life in the direction you want, or not. The key distinction here is that an important task is not necessarily urgent, and an urgent task is not necessarily important. Often the opposite is true. The more urgent a task, the less important it tends to be, and the more important a task, the less urgent it tends to be. In other words, just because a task has a deadline doesn't mean it should be done immediately, or for that matter, done at all. And just because a task comes without a deadline does not mean that you should automatically put it off in favor of one that comes with a deadline.

To illustrate the point for yourself, make a list of all the tasks you have to perform tomorrow. Then place each task into one of these four categories:

Category 1: Both urgent and important
Category 2: Important, but not urgent
Category 3: Urgent, but not important
Category 4: Neither important nor urgent

If a task falls into Category 1, place a "1" beside it. If it falls into Category 3, place a "3" beside it, and so on until you've labeled every item on your list. Once you have finished labeling your tasks, notice how many of them fall into Category 3 (Urgent).

For many of us, urgency is a disease. Once a task has been given a deadline, it occupies our attention far out of proportion to its merits. When someone asks us to do something "as soon as possible," we tend to put that item at the top of our list, whether it deserves to be there or not. If the person making the request happens to be our boss, then that might justify turning a merely urgent task into an important task. But if the person making the request is not our boss, then chances are the task we are being asked to perform right away is not as important to us as it is to the person who is asking us to do it. So when we work on that item first, we are letting someone else set our agenda, an agenda that contradicts our own. We are letting someone else determine how we spend that precious and irreplaceable resource called time. That's not the way to make your wish come true.

Wishes—and the tasks that constitute them—typically fall into Category 2. They are important. They take us where we want to go. They give us what we want most from life. But typically, they aren't urgent. They don't have to be performed this instant. So all too often, these important tasks are pushed aside in favor of tasks that are more urgent, but less important. The busyness of living crowds out the things we live for. This is a classic example of time mismanagement, and one of the primary causes of failure. But how can we prevent this?

If you want to make your wish come true, spend your time in Category 2. Work on the important tasks, the ones that will take you where you want to go. Let the merely urgent tasks take care of themselves. Most of them will simply go away. And those that don't will have to be scheduled around more important tasks, instead of the other way around.

Big Rocks

Imagine that you're sitting in one of my seminars with several hundred other people. I'm standing at the front of the room, behind a table on which sits a large glass jar. I begin to fill the jar with rocks. When I've put in as many rocks as the jar will hold, I turn to the group and ask, "Is the jar full?" Dozens of voices answer, "Yes!"

But of course the jar isn't full. I begin to pour in cup after cup of gravel. The gravel insinuates itself into the empty spaces between the big rocks. When the jar won't hold any more gravel I turn to the group and ask, "Is the jar full?" This time only a few voices answer, "Yes!"

But of course the jar isn't full. I begin to dump in cup after cup of sand. The sand fills every nook and cranny left by the rocks and the gravel. When the jar won't hold any more sand I turn to the group and ask, "Is the jar full?" This time nobody seems to know what to say. They look at one another hoping that the other guy might know the correct answer. Finally, a couple of people timidly respond, "No."

And they're right—the jar isn't full. I begin to pour in glass after glass of water. The water fills the space that remains between the grains of sand until eventually, the jar overflows. Once more I turn to the group and ask, "Is the jar full?" They just stare at me, waiting for whatever comes next.

That's when I break the good news: At last, the jar is full. Then I ask, "What is the moral of this story?"

Immediately, someone volunteers, "The moral is that there is always room to squeeze at least one more task into your day if you just keep trying."

A reasonable enough conclusion, but not the one I was looking for. The point of the demonstration is that there will be no room for big rocks unless you put them in first. If you put in the sand, and gravel, and water first, you won't be able to fit any big rocks at all.

The same holds true for scheduling your activities. If you allow your days to become filled with the details and trivia of modern life—the sand, gravel, and water—you'll never have time for the tasks you consider most important, the big rocks of Category 2. If you don't schedule your big rocks first, your schedule will fill up with less important tasks, and you will never find the time to do the things that will make your wish come true.

As for the other categories of tasks, Category 4 speaks for itself. The tasks in this category are neither important nor urgent. I call this kind of activity "puttering." Some people spend their lives puttering. They are always busy but they never seem to accomplish anything. Spending time in this category is not a good prescription for making your wish come true.

A Category 1 task is both urgent and important. You have to drop whatever you're doing and get the Category 1 task done. There is a name for this kind of task: it's called a crisis. If you find yourself jumping from crisis to crisis, you're spending too much time in Category 1. Again, this is not a good prescription for making your wishes come true. The way to beat this crisis syndrome is to spend more time in Category 2, working on tasks that are important, before they have a chance to become urgent.

For example, suppose you want to lose enough weight to fit into a bathing suit by next summer. That's a Category 2 task. It's important to you to lose the weight, but it's not urgent. You have a whole year to make that wish come true, so why worry about diet and exercise right now? What's the rush? But come next spring, if you're still as heavy as you are today, then you're going to find that losing all that weight by summer has suddenly become a crisis. The task has moved into Category 1 because you didn't pay attention to it while it was in Category 2.

When you do first things first, when you complete important tasks before they become urgent, you spend less of your time fighting fires, and more of your time getting things done. That is what time management is all about. And that is a great prescription for making your wish come true.

11 *Problems*

Problems are a sign of life. The only people without problems are those who are already buried six feet underground. So don't wish for fewer problems, wish for more skill in solving them.

Problems exist because there are far more ways for things to go wrong than for things to go right. You can misspell a word a hundred ways, but there is just one way to spell it right. You can give a thousand wrong answers to a math problem, but there is just one right answer. There are more ways to clutter your house than to keep it clean. There are more ways to lose a sale than to make one.

Making your wishes come true is a matter of solving whatever problems stand in your way. At birth, you were given the most powerful problem-solving computer in the world: a human brain. The trick to solving any problem is to persuade that brain to do what it does best—*think*.

What follows is a three-step thinking process that will help you solve any problem you encounter:

1. Decide what problem you want to solve.
2. Choose the solution.
3. Take action to implement your solution.

The last of these steps requires little explanation. We've talked enough about taking action to know that nothing happens until you act, until you begin to set in motion the causes of the effects you desire. So let's focus on the first two steps.

Step 1. Decide what problem you want to solve.

Suppose you wake up Monday morning after a two-week vacation, start to get dressed, and discover you've gained so much weight that none of your clothes fit. Which of these is the real problem?

a. Your body is too big.
b. Your clothes are too small.
c. You don't have anything to wear to work.

The answer: They are all real problems. You can't even begin to think about a solution until you decide which of these problems you want to solve. If you decide to solve all three of them, you have to decide which one you're going to solve first.

Step 2. Choose the solution.

There is more than one way to solve a problem. For example, if you don't have anything to wear to work, you can race out and buy some new clothes. Or you can borrow some clothes. Or you can make some clothes. Or you can quit.

The solution you choose to any problem depends on the result you want to produce. For instance, if you find yourself in an unhappy marriage, you have to decide whether you want to save your marriage or get out of it. If you have a dead-end job, you have to decide whether you want a promotion, or a transfer, or a new employer. If your car breaks down, you have to decide whether you want to fix it or buy another car. Once you choose the result you want, you enable yourself to choose a course of action that will cause that result to happen.

Brainstorming Session

You can come up with a whole range of solutions for even your toughest problems if you think of a solution as nothing more than an answer to an appropriate question. Just ask yourself the question and listen to your answers. Sound familiar? It should. It's the same brainstorming process we covered in chapter 1. Here's how you can apply that five step process to help you solve any problem you encounter:

> *1. Write the problem you want to solve in the form of a question at the top of a clean sheet of paper.*

To tap the problem-solving power of your own mind, you have only to ask it a question and then listen to your answers.

2. Write whatever pops into your head.

Ask yourself the question you've written at the top of your page, then write every answer that springs to mind.

3. Accept with gratitude whatever pops into your head.

Your brain is a gold mine, or as I like to think of it, a *gold mind*. Mine it for all it's worth. Accept every thought as if it were a nugget of pure gold.

Trust yourself. Your most bizarre ideas may, in the light of day, prove to be your best. Or your best ideas may be lurking just behind an outrageous thought, and you have to drag that outrageous thought out of your mind, and out of the way, before you can get to the real gold.

4. Keep your pen moving.

Tell yourself you're going to brainstorm for two minutes, or five minutes, or whatever. Then keep your pen moving until the time is up.

5. Save your criticism for later.

Write, don't judge. You'll have plenty of time later to judge.

When you have completed your brainstorming session, you will have a list of possible solutions to the problem you wrote at the top of your paper. You can then decide which solutions you want to pursue and file the rest.

The more you practice brainstorming, the better you'll

become. Before you know it, you'll be able to reel off bankable solutions as easily as you can recite the days of the week.

Look for Two Solutions

There are at least two solutions for any problem, and probably a great many more. Once you find one solution, keep looking for another, and then another. Keep your mind open. Instead of telling yourself to look for that one perfect solution, tell yourself to look for the best solution among alternatives. Then keep looking for alternatives. Keep asking yourself questions. Keep listening to your answers. As long as you do, your mind will continue to serve them up on a silver platter.

Look for the Obvious

Urban legend has it that once during a rush hour in New York City, a tractor-trailer became stuck in the Holland Tunnel. The truck was too tall to move forward and wedged too tightly to move backward. The police, already on the scene, called in the fire department. They drew all their best minds together to consider the problem and came up with what seemed like the only logical solution: saw off the top of the tractor-trailer and tow the rig out of the tunnel.

Then a car drove by in the opposite lane. Inside, a little girl asked her dad why don't they just let the air out of the truck's tires? Her dad pulled over and asked the police. They scratched their heads, looked embarrassed, and followed the little girl's advice. Within minutes, they had the truck clear of the tunnel.

The little girl was too young and too naive to look for difficult solutions, so she came up with an easy one. Keep that in mind next time you face a tough problem. Look for solutions right under your nose, where they're so obvious you might be inclined to ignore them, like a pair of slacks you can't find in the closet because they're hanging in front of your eyes.

Try a Fresh Perspective

Would you describe the above shape as convex or concave? The answer depends on your perspective. If you're standing to the right of the drawing, it looks concave. If you're standing to the left, it looks convex. Simply by shifting your point of view, you can change one description of "reality" into its exact opposite.

Next time you face a tough problem, try approaching it from a fresh perspective. The problem will take on a whole new meaning and present you with a range of new solutions.

For example, lumber mills used to have an awful time disposing of sawdust. It was inconvenient and expensive. It was also a fact of life for the lumber business, until someone came along and looked at the problem from a fresh perspective. Instead of seeing waste, he saw raw material. Instead of seeing sawdust, he saw Presto Logs. By adding a little wax to the sawdust and a fancy wrapper, he created a new product that made him rich and allowed lumber mills to make money selling sawdust, instead of paying to have it hauled away.

In every "unsolvable" problem is the seed of a solution. To recognize that solution, all you have to do is to look at the problem in a new light. Come at each of your problems from a fresh perspective and you will be able to create no end of fresh solutions.

What If?

What if the next time you hear yourself say, "That will never work," you quickly add, *But what if I try it anyway*? When you ask *What if?* you allow yourself to consider all your options, to try them on for size, without risk. You open yourself to possibilities that would otherwise remain hidden from you. You allow yourself to explore all the potential solutions to a problem, instead of just the ones that seem politically correct. Armed with more choices, you improve your chances of making the right one.

Give Yourself Advice

Another great way to come up with creative solutions is to ask yourself this question: "If I happened upon someone with the same problem I am trying to solve, what advice would I give to that person?"

For example, suppose you would like to change careers. You want to start over in a new field that interests you, instead of spending the rest of your life in the same mind-numbing business you stumbled into when you finished school. But you have a family to support, bills to pay, a mortgage check to write every month. How can you make the switch from one career to another without giving up your standard of living?

To answer this question, pretend you're riding in an airplane and you strike up a conversation with the person sitting beside you. He tells you he's dying to change careers, but he can't afford to give up his standard of living. What advice would you give him?

Would you tell him to make the change, or else in ten years he'll find himself exactly where he is now? Would you tell him he will perform so much better in a job he loves than in a job he hates, that he will actually raise his standard of living? Would you tell him that finding fulfillment and happiness in life is more important than buying a new car every three years? Would you tell him that life is too short to waste in the wrong career? Sure you would! You would tell him all these things because it's easier to give advice than it is to follow it.

Following good advice is hard work—too hard for most of us, so all too often we tend to hide our best advice from ourselves. To get the benefit of our own best advice, sometimes we have to pretend we're giving that advice to someone else.

Don't Even Think About It

I call my wife so often at her office that I dial her number without thinking. But if you asked me her number—if you asked me to think about it—I would have to dial it to answer your question.

Remember when you learned how to drive a car? First you had to learn the rules of the road—right of way, speed limits, safe-driving tips. Then you had to learn how to operate your vehicle. You had to master the steering wheel, the transmission, the gas pedal, the brakes. Then, probably in a parking lot, you had to practice using all of these unfamiliar controls in unison, preferably without driving the car through the side of a building. Finally, you had to put it all together on a real highway and somehow maneuver a 3,000-pound projectile from point A to point B, while hundreds of other similar projectiles raced by you at 60 miles an hour. All without killing yourself or your poor driving instructor, all while keeping in mind everything you had just learned about safe driving.

Of course, you couldn't keep it all in mind, at least not consciously. You weren't any good at driving until you learned to drive unconsciously. The better your driving, the more unconscious your driving skills became. Within weeks, not only were you able to cruise comfortably at the speed limit, but far beyond it—with a Coke in one hand, a hamburger in the other, and your free arm around your date, all the while chatting happily with the couple in the backseat.

There is more about you than meets the eye. The most powerful part of your mind, the part responsible for your skills, your emotions, your memory, and your deepest thinking, is subconscious. Most of you is below the surface. You might not know it's there, and you might not know what it's doing, but it's running the show—your show. Your subconscious mind is the single most powerful tool you can command to solve problems. To unleash this power, you have only to learn how to let your subconscious do your thinking for you.

Have you ever taken a test where you knew an answer, but you couldn't remember it while you were sitting in the classroom? Then the bell rang, you walked out the door, and the answer popped into your head. Your subconscious finally got around to giving you the answer once you let go of the question. Therein lies the secret to tapping the power of the subconscious. Let go of the question with your conscious mind, and your subconscious mind will provide the answer.

Your best thinking is done subconsciously. That's why we get so many of our best ideas at the strangest times—in the shower, just before we drop off to sleep, driving to work, wolfing down a steak sub—while our conscious mind is preoccupied with other things.

To put your subconscious mind to work solving problems, follow these three steps:

1. Turn your problem into a question, and then ask yourself the question.

For example, if the problem you are trying to solve is that you can't stop falling asleep at work, you might ask yourself, *How can I stay alert and energized all day long?*

2. Once you have asked yourself the question, let go of it and turn your attention to something else.

Your answer may not come for hours, or even days. But don't worry, it will come. If you *do* worry, it may not come. It may hover in the wings, like an actor afraid to appear on stage, until you turn your attention somewhere else.

If you don't come up with an answer within two or three days, ask yourself the question again, and then let go of it again. Repeat this cycle for as long as it takes to get your question answered. Trust your subconscious. Expect answers, and they will come.

3. Write your answers the moment they come to you.

Ideas are like lottery tickets you can print for yourself. You just keep printing them until you win. But you can't cash these ideas in unless you have written them down.

When you commit your thoughts to paper, you let your subconscious know you're listening, so it's more inclined to give you something to listen to. If you ignore what it gives you, it will stop giving it to you.

When you commit your thoughts to paper the moment they occur, you capture ideas that would otherwise vanish into your subconscious, like a fish slips off a hook and disappears into the sea. If you think an idea will hang around for a day, or an hour, or even a few minutes, until you find the time to write it down you're fooling yourself, and you're throwing away your most valuable resource. The weakest ink is mightier than the most powerful memory. Whatever you write down, you cannot forget. If you put your thoughts in writing before they leave you, they will never leave you.

I keep a pad of paper and a pen everywhere I go—in my car, my bathroom, my briefcase, beside my bed, in my pocket—just in case I get an idea. I don't want to lose even a single idea because I lacked the good sense to write it down. Nothing is more powerful than an idea whose time has come; nothing is more useless than an idea whose time has come and gone because it was forgotten. An idea is a terrible thing to waste—*write it down.*

There is no better time to ask yourself a problem-solving question than just before you fall asleep because we do some of our best thinking while we sleep. That's why, when we face a tough decision, we decide to "sleep on it."

When you ask yourself a question at bedtime, let go of it. Let the answer come in its own good time. Enjoy your sleep in the relaxed assurance that the answer will be waiting for you in the morning. If you think about your question consciously, you will only keep yourself awake. But if you sleep on it, you will let your subconscious do the work while you rest the night away.

Like anything else you want to master, the process of tapping your subconscious mind will take some practice, but the practice is easy. All you have to do is to ask yourself a question and record the answers when they come. The more you exercise your problem-solving muscles, the stronger they become, and the better they become at solving the problems that stand between you and making your wish come true.

Step 3. Take Action

Once you've determined what problem you're going to solve and then chosen the appropriate solution, the next thing you need to do is take action to implement your solution. Action makes the difference between those who solve problems, and those who are problems.

When it comes to facing a problem, there are two types of people in the world: those who ask, "Why me?" and those who ask, "What am I going to do about it?" In this question lies the difference between the great and the ingrate, the champion and the chump, the winner and the whiner.

As I've said before, any idiot can tell you what's wrong with the world. The movers and shakers do something about it. The best solution in the world won't solve a problem unless you take the action necessary to put that solution to work. Act, and you will solve the problem. Don't act, and you will become the problem.

12 *Help*

You alone are responsible for making your wishes come true. You alone are the one who has to make things happen. You alone make or break your own success. But your greatest resource is other people.

Whatever effort you make on your own, you can multiply by enlisting the help of other people. Other people have resources you don't have: a different point of view, different ideas, different skills, different experiences, different contacts, a different checking account. When you enlist other people in your cause, their resources become your resources.

The people you already know can help you ask for help from literally anyone in the country. For example, suppose you're a high school student and you want to ask a favor of the president of the United States. First, you would talk to someone you already know—a teacher, your school principal, a coach, or perhaps the owner of the business where you work during summer vacation. Let's assume that you've decided to approach the business owner. Chances are that he or she knows many of the leading citizens of your community. One of these leading citizens most likely knows the congressman from your area. You can be sure that your congressman has the clout to place a phone call to the president of the United States.

Your plan of action would be to ask the business owner, to ask the community leader, to ask the congressman, to ask the president for a favor on your behalf. Four steps, and you're at the very top. If you can reach the president this easily, you can reach anyone else you care to reach.

Think of someone who might help you make your wish come true. If you've written a book, you might want to contact a publisher. If you're trying to land your dream job, you might want to reach the person who is hiring. If you're trying to get your big break as an actor, you might want to reach a Hollywood producer. If you want to become a roadie for your favorite rock-and-roll band, you might want to reach the band's manager. If you're trying to get into graduate school, you might want to reach the director of admissions. Think of anyone in the country (or the world, for that matter), and then think of how you might reach that person through the people you already know.

For instance, suppose you want to have your résumé considered by the one person in the world who can hire you for your dream job. Let's say this person happens to be a vice president of the CBS Television Network. Think of someone you know who works for CBS. If you don't know anyone, think of someone you know who might know someone who works for CBS (at the local CBS affiliate station, for example). Once you make contact with someone who works for CBS, you'll find that he or she knows somebody (a boss, or a boss's boss, perhaps) who knows somebody (an executive) who knows the vice president you're trying to reach. It's that simple. In fact, the more successful the person you want to reach, the more people he or she knows, so the easier it is to reach that person through other people.

People can help you in so many ways. They can give you advice, training, money, feedback, contacts, and emotional support. They can make the difference between spectacular success and lonely failure. They can give you everything you need to make your wish come true. There's just one catch: If you want help you're going to have to ask for it. When you do, you will want to stack the deck in your favor. Below is a five-step strategy that will help you earn a *Yes* when you ask for something instead of a *No*.

1. Ask for something specific.

The best way to help someone help you is to be specific about what you're asking for. If your helper doesn't know exactly what you want, how can he or she help you get it? For that matter, if you don't know exactly what you want, how can you ask for it?

Help your helper help you. If you force him to fill in the

blanks, he'll probably fill them in wrong. Or he might not help you at all because he doesn't understand what you want. If you don't understand, how can he?

Be specific. If you're asking for money, ask for exactly the amount you need and when you need it. If you're asking for an introduction to someone, specify who, and when, and exactly what you want your helper to say on your behalf. If you're asking for advice, ask your advisor for a specific solution to a specific problem. If you're asking for emotional support, ask for precisely the kind of support you need. If you aren't specific about what you ask for, you won't get it.

2. Ask someone who can help you get it.

Before you ask for something, first ask yourself this question: *Can this person give me what I want?* If the answer is *No,* then find someone who can.

If you want money, ask someone who can give it to you or can help you get it. If you want a promotion or a new job, ask someone who can promote you, or hire you, or put you in touch with someone who can. If you want to sell something, ask someone who has the power to buy it. If you want to buy something, ask someone who has the power to sell it. When you go to the trouble to ask for something, make sure you ask someone who can give it to you.

Nowhere is this more important—and more misunderstood—than when it comes to asking for advice. Our first tendency is to ask for advice from the people we know best.

Too often, they are more than willing to help but are less than helpful.

For example, we ask our parents how to become wealthy, although they have never become wealthy themselves. We ask our best friend how to get a promotion, although he can't hold a job. We ask our neighbor how to lose weight, although she can no longer fit into the dress she bought last week. They all mean well; they just don't know well. They don't know enough about the task at hand to be of help.

Unless someone has already been where you want to go, the chances are that he or she can't tell you how to get there. If you want good advice, ask someone who has already achieved what you want to achieve and can tell you from experience how you can do the same. Ask someone who can help.

3. Make it worthwhile for the person you ask.

People may help you out of love; they may help you out of compassion; but they will definitely help you out of self-interest. If you want someone to help you, make it worth his while.

When you ask for something, the question that is most likely to form in the mind of the person you're asking is this: *What's in it for me?* How you answer that question will largely determine whether or not that person is willing to help you. If you can find a way to sufficiently enrich his life, he will be eager to enrich yours. If you can find a way to serve him, you will be amazed how willingly he serves you. You don't have to convince him, you don't have to persuade him, you don't have to pressure him. You have only to make it worth his while. The rest will take care of itself.

4. Be sincere.

I don't mean *act* sincere; I mean *be* sincere. It's not a matter of how you come across; it's a matter of how you feel. Do you really want what you're asking for? If not, how can you expect someone else to want to give it to you? Are you certain about what you want? If not, the person you're asking for help will be uncertain about giving it to you.

Whenever you feel a conflict on the inside, it shows on the outside. It makes people more likely to resist you than to help you. If you have doubts about what you want, convince yourself first, before you try to convince anyone else. Then, when you're sure about what you want, you can ask for it sincerely, with absolute conviction. The more convinced you are about what you want, the more likely you are to convince someone else to help you get it.

5. Keep asking until you get what you want.

Some people hear the word *no* and give up. Other people hear *no* and think that all they need is a bigger hammer. When they find one, they keep pounding until they hear a *yes*. I don't recommend either approach.

No means that what you're doing isn't working, so try something else. You don't need a hammer; you need a key—the key that will unlock the other person's heart.

Maybe you haven't asked the right question yet. Maybe you haven't made it worth that person's while. Maybe you haven't been specific enough. Maybe you haven't been sincere. Somewhere along the line you haven't done whatever it is you need to do to inspire that person to help you. So try something else. Or try someone else. And keep trying until you get what you want. If you keep trying until you get what you ask for, you will always get what you ask for.

L.A.M.P. Process Step 3:

Manage Your Progress

13 *Focus*

When you were a child did you ever use a magnifying glass to burn your initials into a block of wood? What was it about that glass that turned the gentle warmth of the sun into a heat ray?

In a word, *focus*. Focus means to converge upon a single point. Focused energy can accomplish what that same energy, unfocused, cannot.

Most people are like the sun on a warm day; they radiate their energy broadly, with no particular object in mind. In living out one day, they accomplish little beyond making it to the next.

Successful people are like a magnifying glass. They focus their energy—and their time and their talent—on exactly what they want to achieve. They know that their power is greatest when it's focused on a single point. They are no better than other people; they are no smarter; they are no more worthy. They possess no more time, or energy, or talent. But they are more focused. They use focus to accomplish what seems beyond their power.

If you want to have the broadest effect on your life, focus on the narrowest point. Concentrate your time, your energy, and your talent on making happen the one thing you most want to happen.

Military strategists call this *concentration of force*. They know that the way to win a battle is to meet the enemy with everything you've got at a point where your forces will overwhelm his. When you're wishing, you can think of "the enemy" as whatever obstacle stands between you and making your wish come true. Focus allows you to concentrate all of your effort on overwhelming that obstacle.

Focus means you put your wish first, ahead of all the other things that compete for your time and attention. You give your wish a half hour, or an hour, or two hours every day—whatever you've set aside for it—before the day slips away, and then the month, and then the year, and you have nothing to show for it. It's not that you have to give up everything else in your life, but you refuse to let everything else distract you from your wish. That's the power of focus.

Keep Your Wish in Front of You

To keep your efforts focused on your wish, keep your wish in front of you. Some people like to post their wish where they'll see it every day—on their bathroom mirror, on the dashboard of their car, atop their computer screen. Others prefer to write their wish on a card and keep the card in their wallet. Whenever they have a free moment during the day—waiting for the subway, when they've been put on hold, standing in line at the checkout counter—they can pull out the card and read their wish.

One thing that works especially well is to write your wish every day instead of reading it. Writing it over and over burns it into your mind and gives you ample incentive to strip away every unnecessary word. The shorter the wish, the greater the emotional impact.

Affirm Your Wish

The most effective way I've found to keep myself focused on the wish at hand is to repeat it every day, like an affirmation. I repeat it aloud, with intense emotion, until I feel it sink in. The number of repetitions isn't nearly as important as the intensity of the emotion.

I say my wish-affirmation at the same time and in the same place every day—in my car on the way to the office. By doing so, I've made it a habit. Each morning when I slide behind the wheel, the first thing I think about is my wish. I find myself repeating it automatically. It gets my morning off to a great start because I know I will spend the entire day focused on making my wish come true.

Another way I keep my wish in front of me is to make a weekly progress report. These reports are built into my L.A.M.P.

Plan, and scheduled on my weekly calendar. I record how much progress I've made during the past week and compare it to what I expected to make. This keeps me focused on my milestones and deadlines, and lets me make adjustments to my plan before it's too late to meet my deadlines.

In the rush of your busy schedule, you might be tempted to skip your progress reports. After all, you know how much progress you're making, right? Wrong. If you skip your progress reports, don't be surprised to find yourself a month, six months, or a year down the road only to realize you're on the wrong road. If you've got that kind of time to waste, by all means skip the reports. But if you want to make every day count, track your progress and stay on top of your L.A.M.P. Plan. That will keep you focused as nothing else can.

One Wish at a Time

If you write your wish every day, affirm it every day, and make a progress report every week, you'll find it exceptionally empowering. If you try to do all of this with several wishes at once, you'll find it exceptionally tedious.

Wishing works because wishing is work. If you pile on too much of that kind of work, you can lose your edge and your enthusiasm. Don't make your life a chore; make it a joy. Work on one wish at a time. Power comes from focus; focus comes from priorities. So set your priorities. Decide what is the most important thing for you to accomplish and work on that until you accomplish it. Once you have completed that wish, you'll be free to work on the next one, and the next one, and then the one after that, until one day you'll look back and see behind you a shimmering trail of all the dreams you've made come true.

Refocus

An airliner flying from New York to Los Angeles is off course 95 percent of the time. The pilot spends most of the flight making adjustments to put the plane back on course.

That's how you can expect to spend most of your time, too, when you're in the process of making a wish come true. Conditions will change, your L.A.M.P. Plan will change, your wish itself may change, and you will confront every imaginable distraction. With all this going on, you will find yourself off course most of the time. Don't beat yourself up about it: refocus. Make the necessary adjustments. Keep making adjustments—focus, refocus, and refocus again—until you reach your destination.

That's the secret of being in it for the long haul: you can refocus whenever you need to. Successful people aren't successful because they're always on track; they're successful because they can always get back on track. They know how to refocus, no matter how far off course they might get.

Luck

Like a television set, your mind can tune in to what interests you and ignore the rest. There is far more happening around you than you have the time or the inclination to pay attention to. You don't notice every knickknack on every desk, every speck of dust on every carpet, every piece of paper in every wastebasket. You don't listen to every snippet of every conversation or every word the announcer is saying on the radio or TV that's playing in the background. You ignore the things that aren't important to you so you can concentrate on the things that are.

Focus is the way you tell your brain what requires attention. Once you tune your brain into a particular channel—by focusing on your wish, for example—you begin to notice all sorts of things around you that you didn't know were there.

You begin to notice resources you didn't know you had. Your best friend, it turns out, knows a woman who can get you that job interview you want. Your neighbor owns a cabin in the woods where you can go to write your novel. Rummaging through the attic, you come across your old stamp collection and realize you can sell it to raise the seed money you need to open your part-time business. An old friend calls to ask you to lunch and happens to be just the person you need to help you solve a problem that has you stumped.

You begin to notice coincidences. Sitting beside you on an airplane is the key contact you've been looking for to help you move your wish along. You thumb through a magazine and find an article that tells you exactly what you need to know to complete the next step in your L.A.M.P. Plan. You attend a party and find yourself being introduced to a woman of influence who can help you grant your wish. You're channel surfing on Sunday morning and happen across a talk show interview with a person who has accomplished exactly what you want to accomplish and is explaining how to go about it. The world calls this "luck." I call it focus.

Have you ever envied someone who was lucky enough to be in the right place at the right time? Who knows how often you've been at the right place at the right time, and never recognized it because you lacked focus? When you don't know what you want, you miss all the opportunities that will help you get it. But when you do know what you want, when you're focused, every place is the right place; every time is the right time.

When you focus on your wish, the whole world comes into focus around you. Lucky breaks converge on you like friends converge on a keg party. You invite all the resources at your command, and all those you didn't know you could command, to help you make your wish come true.

14 *Connection*

Implementing a L.A.M.P. Plan can take weeks, months, or even years to complete. That's a long time to stay up for anything. What do you do when you feel tired, or bored, or worst of all, discouraged?

These feelings are a warning to you that you've lost your emotional connection with your wish. You've become unplugged from the source of your power. You're going through the motions, but you're no longer feeling the emotions. You've lost touch with whatever it was that energized you to pursue your wish in the first place.

You can keep pushing yourself and disciplining yourself, but that's not much fun. Why not spare yourself all that hassle and pain and simply reconnect to your wish? Plug yourself back in to that wall socket of emotion. Don't force yourself to do what's good for you; inspire yourself to do what's good for you.

The secret is to let yourself feel right now the thrill you will eventually feel when you make your wish come true. Enjoy your emotional payoff today instead of waiting until later. Use your emotions to help carry you toward your destination, not just to reward you when you get there. Whatever step you're on—however trivial or tedious it might seem—allow yourself to feel as if you're completing your whole wish.

Enjoy the process. Fall in love with the process the same way you've fallen in love with your wish. Let yourself enjoy every step along the way, no matter how uninspiring any step might be.

For example, if you're training to win the marathon at the Olympics and you're running hundreds of grueling miles every week, you know you're connected to your wish when you feel as though every stride in practice is a joy because it's helping you win the Gold.

If you're looking for work and you've already mailed 200 résumés without receiving a single reply, you know you're connected to your wish when you drop yet another résumé in the mail and feel great because you've just moved one step closer to success.

If you've just opened your own company and you've already lost your third order today because your customers think you're inexperienced, you know you're connected to your wish when you can't wait to call the next prospect. Win or lose, you know that every contact you make will take you one step closer to a thriving business.

When you're emotionally connected to your wish, the payoff is *now.* Not tomorrow. Not next year. Right now. You don't have to delay your gratification. You don't have to wait for your reward. With every step you take, you allow yourself to feel the joy of completion, the thrill of success. You keep your eye on the prize and let yourself savor the prize throughout your journey.

When you're connected to your emotional payoff, your L.A.M.P. Plan can sail the roughest seas. When you're disconnected, your plan can be swamped by the smallest wave.

Preference Questions

Preference questions help you stay connected to your wish. They help you focus your attention and your energy on doing the things today that will help cause your wish to come true tomorrow, even when your natural tendency might be to do just the opposite.

For example, think of your wish as an *ultimate desire* that may from time to time conflict with something you want to do right now—what I call an *immediate desire*. Suppose your ultimate desire is to lose thirty pounds in six months, but your immediate desire is to inhale a hot fudge sundae that is melting in front of your eyes. You know you can put off your ultimate desire, but that hot fudge sundae is right here, right now. You can reach out and touch it, and smell it, and, heaven help you, taste it. Chances are you'll be inclined to satisfy your immediate craving at the expense of your ultimate dream. That's called "human nature."

You can try to overcome human nature, through iron-willed self-discipline and denial, but that's the hardest work on earth. Why not work smarter instead of harder? Instead of forcing ···rself to toe the line, change the line. Make your ultimate desire and your immediate desire change places. Turn the sundae into something you can put off. Then turn your ideal weight into something you insist on right now.

You can make this all-important switch simply by asking yourself a preference question: *At this instant, would I prefer to be at my ideal weight or have a hot fudge sundae?*

Notice that you aren't asking yourself if you would like to reach your ideal weight some time in the future. Instead, you're asking yourself if you would prefer that weight right now, in place of a hot fudge sundae.

Under these circumstances, if you choose the sundae, you might as well give up your wish to lose weight. You have no intention of following through. If you don't prefer your ideal weight to a sundae today, when will you?

But if you choose your ideal weight over a sundae, you're on the right track. You've made an important decision: At this moment, being at my target weight is more important than eating a hot fudge sundae. You've turned an ultimate desire into an immediate desire and given yourself the leverage you need to make your wish come true.

Procrastination

The next step is to turn the hot fudge sundae into something you can put off. You've spent your whole life learning how to procrastinate—why not put it to good use?

Whenever you're tempted to do something now that will set you back later, put it off. Don't deny it. Don't forbid it. Don't threaten yourself. Just procrastinate.

The beauty of procrastination is that there is nothing to resist. There is nothing to rebel against. Instead of saying *No,* you're saying *Later.* When *Later* comes, the urge may have passed. If not, just put it off again. Keep putting it off, and *Later* will never come.

Never underestimate the power of procrastination. You can turn your life around with this single skill, a skill that most of us consider a bad habit. Use this skill to distance yourself from whatever might get in your way, so you're free to reconnect with your wish and enjoy your emotional payoff today.

15 *Flexibility*

If what you're doing isn't working, try something else. If you've tried unsuccessfully to smash through a brick wall, go around it. If you can't go around it, go under it. If you can't go under it, go over it. If you can't go over it, then have it moved. Keep trying new options until one of them works. That's the meaning of flexibility.

When you run out of options, you lose. The trick is to keep looking for alternatives and trying them until you find one that works. The next time you think, *I have no choice,* change your mind. Tell yourself, *I have many choices!* Then explore what those choices might be.

You may be surprised to find that there are always choices, if you're flexible enough to look for them. You just have to keep your mind open to the possibility of success. The moment you close your mind, the moment you stop looking for alternatives, you abandon all the other options that may be available to you, all the other chances you may have for success.

Sometimes you have to create options when you're certain that none exist. That's the easiest time of all. When you can't think of anything that will work, make a list of all the things that won't work. Then for each item on your list ask yourself: *But what if it would?*

When you can't think of anything you *can* do, make a list of all the things you *can't* do. Then for each item on your list ask yourself: *But what if I could?*

Finally, make a list of all the things you could do if only they weren't against the rules. Then think about how you can change the rules.

Rules—what rules? Whenever you tell yourself *I should* or *I shouldn't, I must* or *I can't,* you're reciting rules. These rules may be explicit, like company policies, or they may be implicit, like the social standards of a community. Either way, they have the same effect—they limit your thinking. They allow you to consider only what is permitted instead of what is possible.

The point isn't to race out and violate every rule you can find; rules and laws and moral codes are the threads from which every society weaves its own survival. But sometimes you have to allow yourself to think beyond the confines of the mental box in which you've been placed by your upbringing and by your culture. You need to think for yourself, instead of letting the folks who make the rules think for you. You need to consider which rules serve you and your community and which rules serve only to get in your way.

In a scene from one of the *Star Trek* movies, Captain Kirk was asked how he had performed in the Kobayashi Maru scenario back when he was a cadet at the Star Fleet Academy. The Kobayashi Maru was a simulated battle in which a cadet was placed in command of a starship, surrounded by enemy vessels, and given no chance to defeat his opponents or to escape. It was meant to be a test of character, designed to show how a cadet would react to a no-win scenario.

Kobayashi Maru was unbeatable—until Kirk came along. He refused to accept the no-win scenario, so he reprogrammed the battle computer to give him a chance to win. Instead of playing by the rules, he created new rules. Given no choice but to lose, he created a choice to win.

Kirk wasn't successful because he broke the rules; he was successful because he didn't let the rules break him. He opened his mind to consider what might lie beyond the rules—beyond "acceptable" behavior—and discovered an option that had eluded everyone else. To go where no cadet had gone before, he first had to think what no cadet had thought before. You have to be open to possibilities before you can recognize them as options.

Success is a matter of how many options you give yourself to succeed. If you believe there's always one more option, one more choice, one more idea you haven't tried, then you'll always have at least one more chance for success. That's what flexibility is all about.

If what you're doing isn't working, try something else. Keep trying something else until you get what you want. You can't fail unless you run out of options. You can't run out of options unless you give up.

16   The Right Map

Imagine for a moment that you're trying to find your way around Chicago with a map of New York City. Nothing is where you expect it to be. No matter how hard you look or how far you drive, you can't get where you're trying to go. Frustrated and confused, you call your father to ask for advice. He tells you that you aren't applying yourself so you'd better get down to work. You thank him, head back into the streets, and redouble your efforts. You drive twice as hard and twice as fast, and you get lost twice as quickly.

Desperate, you call a self-help guru. You explain that you can't find a single landmark to guide you. Nothing is where it should be. You're lost, and you don't know what to do.

He says you have a bad attitude. If only you would think positively, everything would turn out all right. You hang up, race to a bookstore, and buy the latest best-seller about positive thinking. You read it and get yourself so pumped up you can't see straight. With fanatical determination, you pull out your trusty map of New York, head back into the streets of Chicago, and search until you drop.

Your L.A.M.P. Plan is nothing more than a road map for success. It will work fine as long as it's the right map. But if you have the wrong map, no matter how hard you try, you'll never get where you want to go.

The next time you find yourself frustrated, exhausted, working your hands to the bone with nothing to show for it, don't try to fix your attitude or your work ethic—fix your map. Here are some questions that will help:

> • *Is your wish presentable?*

Are you going after what you want or what you don't want? Are you specific enough? Are you wishing for something you can control? You know the drill by now; if not, go back through the steps listed in chapter 4 and make certain your wish is presentable.

> • *Is this wish really the most important thing for you to focus on right now?*

Maybe your priorities have changed.

> • *Is this wish really worth the price?*

Maybe the price is higher than you thought, or maybe the pay-off isn't as great as you once imagined.

 • *How will you know when your wish has been granted?*

Maybe you already have what you want but you just haven't noticed.

 • *Are you meeting your milestones?*

Maybe your milestones are unrealistic, or maybe they're the wrong milestones.

 • *Can your L.A.M.P. Plan—your map—take you where you want to go?*

Is every step of your plan one that you can achieve? When all these steps are completed, will they make your wish come true? Have you given yourself enough time? Have you given yourself enough money? Have you given yourself enough of all the other resources you're going to need? If your logic doesn't work or your numbers don't add up, give yourself a break. Revise your plan.

 • *What do you need to do differently?*

If what you're doing isn't working and you keep doing it, you're going to keep getting the same results. If you want different results, try something else.

When you take the time to fix your map, you give yourself a chance to make any adjustments that might be necessary to keep you on track. You reaffirm your commitment to your wish. You allow yourself to catch your breath and return to your wish refreshed and renewed. You refocus your efforts so that all your resources can be brought to bear on whatever is holding you back. Most important, you give yourself the kind of motivation that can come only from certainty—the certainty that the things you're doing are the things that will work.

17 *Going with the Flow*

Some folks say that the only way to make your wishes come true is to work hard. Others say that the only way to make your wishes come true is to go with the flow. These pieces of advice seem to contradict one another. But they are not a contradiction; they are a paradox.

Remember *Kung Fu,* the TV series? A soft-spoken character named Caine wanders the Old West, with no particular purpose, and no particular destination. He's just going with the flow. About forty-five minutes into every show, the flow forces him to fight. He cracks a few skulls, dispenses some sage advice, and then wanders off to the next episode. It's corny, but it can teach you a lot about the paradox of going with the flow.

Caine wasn't some alienated college kid who decided to drop

out of the rat race, carve himself a flute, and then spend the rest of his life living off the land. He was a Shaolin priest. He spent his youth training his body, mind, and spirit in the ancient and grueling rituals of the Shaolin Temple. By the time he reached manhood, he was capable of what the Eastern philosophers call "spontaneous right action." He could afford to go with the flow because he was prepared for whatever it might bring.

Therein lies the paradox: Caine could go with the flow only because he had worked so hard to prepare himself to do so. He had prepared himself for whatever the world might throw at him so he could allow himself to take the world as it would come. He had turned himself into the kind of person for whom the right decision would come naturally, so he could yield to his nature without fearing the consequences. He could trust his instincts without fearing the results because he had forged those instincts through intense self-discipline. He could trust himself to do the right thing, because he had forged himself into the kind of person for whom the right thing would come naturally.

You can do the same thing. If you want to spend your life doing whatever comes naturally to you, first, you must create the kind of nature that will bring you what you want. You must fashion the habits of mind, body, and spirit that will enable you to make your wishes come true. You must turn yourself into the kind of person that the flow just naturally takes wherever you want to go, like an actor who has learned his lines so well he no longer has to worry about what he says, he simply acts. At that point, your wishes become a natural expression of who you are, and making those wishes come true becomes as natural as breathing.

When you take the time and make the effort for this kind of

preparation, you prepare yourself to enjoy the most gratifying rewards life has to offer. You prepare yourself to take life as it comes. You prepare yourself to relax and let your instincts take over. You prepare yourself to go with the flow. Just remember that you have to work as hard as a Shaolin priest to get there.

18 *Struggle*

When you find yourself working hard to make a wish come true but nothing seems to be going your way, sooner or later you are going to ask yourself: Why do I have to work so hard to get what I want? Why is life such a struggle?

Entropy

We can find a useful answer to those questions by taking a look at a natural phenomenon that physicists call *entropy*. Think of entropy as the tendency of everything in the world to deteriorate. Paint peels from the side of a building. Ice melts. The tallest mountains are worn to rolling hills. Bridges rust. Roads develop potholes. Even the mightiest ancient pyramid, over time, will crumble to dust. This tendency to unravel is at the heart of the natural universe. No wonder, then, that this same tendency is at the very heart of our own lives.

Think about it. There are more ways for something to go wrong than there are for something to go right. It is far easier to waste time than it is to put time to productive use. Money can slip through our hands more easily than it can be accumulated. It's a lot easier to allow ourselves to go to pot than it is to stay in tiptop physical condition. Entropy means that we can putter away ours days, which turn into months, which turn into years, and before we know it we find ourselves at the end of our lives without having accomplished anything more important than our own survival. We struggle against entropy every day of our lives. And that is why wishing is so important.

Wishing is the opposite of entropy. Wishing makes everything come together; entropy makes everything fall apart. Wishing is an organizing principle; entropy is a disorganizing principle. Wishing enables us to focus our time, our energy, and our talent on what we most want to accomplish, instead of allowing these invaluable resources to slip away. Wishing overcomes entropy by replacing the infinite distractions of daily life with a purpose. Then our time and our effort can tend toward fulfilling that purpose, instead of being squandered on the trivia of daily life.

Where entropy merely passes the time, wishing puts our time to work. Where entropy sucks the life from us, wishing infuses us with meaning, energy, and a sense of mission. Where entropy dissipates our time and effort until we have nothing left, wishing invests these resources in meaningful work so that we have something to show for them.

When we make a wish, we reverse the process of entropy. We focus our time, our energy, and our talent on what we want to accomplish, instead of frittering our lives away. We accept the fact that life is a struggle and thus we free ourselves to stop asking "Why?" and start asking *What am I going to do about it?* When we no longer major in minor things, we allow ourselves to focus on the things that really matter. We grant ourselves the power to make our wishes come true.

The Benefit of Struggle

Now that you understand why life is such a struggle, think about what that struggle can do for you.

Struggle presents you with the opportunity to become more than what you are. Everything you are as a person, you had to become. And chances are you had to do it through struggle. You weren't born knowing how to talk, or how to walk, or even how to think. You had to work at these skills. You didn't just learn them, you had to earn them. By struggling to master them, you became the kind of person for whom such skills were possible.

Imagine what would have happened if you hadn't had to struggle. Suppose that on the day you entered high school you had been given the power to have anything you wanted from life—without having to earn it. If that had been the case, by today you would be no further along mentally, emotionally, or physically than you were when you were a freshman in high school. You would have none of the skills you have now. You would have none of the success. You would have none of the failures, nor would you have learned the invaluable lessons those failures taught. You would be a textbook case of what psychologists call arrested development. Quit literally, you would not be the person you are today. You would not have the knowledge you now have; you would not have the maturity; you would not have presence of mind. You wouldn't even have the same personality.

Thank goodness the world doesn't work that way. In real life, we have to earn what we learn. In the process of learning, we become better people. We become more accomplished people. We become more capable people, because the more we *have* accomplished, the more we *can* accomplish. Scientists call this a positive feedback loop. The rest of us call it growth. And growth is the payoff from struggle.

Struggle makes us stronger. Struggle makes us better. Struggle makes us who we are. Without struggle, we would never be forced to exceed our limits, to stretch ourselves, to achieve our potential. We would never be forced to search for the best within ourselves—and find it. Without struggle, we would never become the kind of people who can make our wishes come true.

19 *Attitude*

Over and over again, we hear the same thing: *Attitude is everything*. You can hardly turn a page in a self-help book without encountering some platitude about attitude. You can't listen to an audiocassette or attend a seminar without hearing a sermon about attitude. And if you read success stories about people who have gotten what they want from life, in example after example, in story after story, attitude emerges as that single, crucial difference between those who make it in life, and those who do not. Everywhere we look, we are surrounded by evidence of the power of attitude. But does it ever sink in?

Look around you. How many people do you know who consistently exhibit a great attitude? Let's turn that around. How many people do you know who have a poor attitude? How many people do you know who complain? How many people do you know who are unhappy? How many people do you know who are anxious, worried, or chronically afraid? These conditions are all examples of a bad attitude. All describe self-inflicted wounds that in turn infect everything they touch. And they all have something in common—they tend to create what they anticipate. In other words, we tend to get what we expect from life, and what we expect is simply a matter of attitude.

Put simply, your attitude determines how effective you will be at making your wishes come true. A good attitude will yield good results. A mediocre attitude will yield mediocre results. A lousy attitude will yield lousy results.

That said, what can you do if you just happen to have a bad attitude? Can you snap your fingers and change your attitude from bad to good? Some self-help gurus would have you believe just that. And they're right, to a point. You can change your actions in the snap of a finger. You can change your facial expression, your posture, even what you're thinking about. And once you change those things, your attitude will change.

But the problem most people have is deeper than that. At any given moment, most of us are simply not thinking about attitude. Our attitude is simply a matter of habit, like posture and breathing, and we take it for granted, just like any other habit. We have the power to change our attitude if we think about it—just as we have the power to change our posture and our breathing if we think about them—but left to our own devices, we shift into autopilot and cop the same attitude we always do. We react to the world the way we have programmed ourselves to do, and we keep on getting the same results we always do. Unless we change our programming—our habits—we will never change our results.

To change your habitual attitude, you have to change your habits of thought and action. You have to change how you habitually react to circumstances. How? The same way you learned everything else you know how to do: through repetition and practice.

Think of your attitude as a skill, instead of as an emotion. You can't control your emotions, at least not directly, but you can control what you do and what you think. So instead of focusing on your feelings, focus on what you need to do and what you need to think in order to produce the results you seek, the same way you did when you learned to ride a bike or throw a Frisbee. Your actions and your thoughts will, in turn, set the tone for your emotions, and thus your attitude.

So don't worry about feeling positive. Concentrate on acting positive, and thinking positive. Practice acting and thinking in positive ways instead of negative ways. Instead of crying over spilt milk, clean it up. Instead of worrying about the cards you've been dealt, play them. Instead of feeling sorry for yourself, do something about it. Don't worry about how you feel, worry about what you do, and what you think.

At first, all this might not come naturally to you. What skills do? The first time out, did writing feel natural? Did reading? Did riding a bicycle? Of course not. But once you practiced these skills enough, they became second nature to you. They became so automatic that you no longer had to think about what you were doing, you just did it.

You can accomplish the same thing with your attitude. Just

keep practicing positive thoughts and actions until they become second nature. For example, from now on why not think of struggle as an opportunity to improve? Why not think of every problem you encounter as a chance to practice your problem-solving skills? The next time you're facing a crisis, practice the skill of focusing your thoughts on the solution, instead of on the problem. Any idiot can tell you what's wrong—and most do—but successful people take action to make it right. If you start thinking and acting that way, everything else will fall into place. And before you know it, making your wishes come true will seem like the most natural thing in the world.

L.A.M.P. Process Step 4:

Persist

20 Persistence

How many times will a baby try to take its first step before it gives up?

A baby doesn't know how to give up. A baby doesn't know the difference between success and failure. It doesn't understand self-discipline. It doesn't know anything about courage. All a baby knows is what it wants, and it keeps going until it gets it. What if you had the same approach to life?

Getting what you want boils down to a single word: *persistence*. No matter how presentable your wish, how good your plan, how tireless your work, your success will ultimately hinge on persistence. Are you willing to go the distance? Then you will succeed. Are you willing to endure when others are ready to quit? Then you will succeed. Are you willing to pursue what you want until you get it, however long it takes? Then you will succeed. Success belongs to those who refuse to settle for less. Persist until you get what you want, and you will always get what you want.

I'm not talking about the grit-your-teeth macho kind of persistence that you read about in most self-help books. Let other people brace themselves like mighty oaks; oaks are often snapped like matchsticks before a strong wind.

The persistence I'm suggesting is the kind that outlasts whatever tries to challenge it. Armed with such persistence, you bend like a reed before the wind. And when the wind passes, you remain. Your purpose remains. And your wish prevails.

Next to persistence, your skills, intelligence, and talents amount to little. The most skillful person who gives up will always finish behind the most inept person who does not. The most intelligent person who gives up will always finish behind the most simple-minded person who does not. The most talented person who gives up will always finish behind the least talented person who does not. The most gifted person alive, if he or she gives up, will always finish behind someone—behind anyone—who does not.

Belief

The most common reason we give up is that we no longer believe in what we're doing. Either we don't believe our effort can succeed or we don't believe that success is worth our effort. Either way, once we lose our belief, we lose our will to continue.

And who can blame us? Why should we plant a garden unless we believe it will bear fruit? Why should we build a house unless we believe it will provide shelter? Why should we undertake personal sacrifice unless we believe that our efforts have a chance of succeeding? Why should we even get out of bed in the morning unless we believe that something worthwhile will come from the day? Without belief, there will be no effort. Without effort, there will be no results.

Belief is the foundation of persistence. Without belief, you have no reason to complete a task. But with belief, you have no reason to quit.

Whenever you find yourself tempted to give up on a wish, ask yourself these questions:

1. Do I believe I can make this wish come true?
2. Do I believe this wish is worth the effort?

If either answer is no, then you need to work on your belief before you can effectively work on your wish. Belief causes persistence. Persistence causes success.

21 *Wish Killers*

By now you have the whole world going for you. You've locked on to your wish; you're taking the appropriate action; you're managing your progress; and you're ready to persist in your efforts until you make your wish come true.

But there may yet be forces at work inside you that can make it difficult or even impossible for you to succeed. I call them *wish killers* because left unchecked that is exactly what they will do.

Fear

The first wish killer is fear. Fear is a negative wish. The more you focus on what you fear, the more likely you are to make it happen.

The human mind does not distinguish between a mental picture of something you want and a mental picture of something you're trying to avoid. The more clearly you picture what you want, the harder your mind will work to give it to you. The more clearly you picture what you're trying to avoid, the harder your mind will work to give you that instead. Whatever you consistently picture on the inside, your mind will do its best to reproduce on the outside. Unless you want to make your fears come true, think of something else.

I learned that when I was a little boy. Like most youngsters, I was afraid of shots, so I had to find some way to control my panic when my Mom led me into the doctor's office. I learned to think about things I really enjoyed—like Disneyland, and birthday presents, and chocolate sundaes—anything to get my mind off what was about to happen. It was a silly little trick, but it worked. It still works, for all kinds of fears. And now I know why.

When you're afraid, the movie you're running in your mind is likely to be a gut-wrenching feature presentation of what you fear. You react to that movie the same way you react to a good horror movie—with sweaty palms, a churning stomach, a racing heart. Change the movie, and you change your reaction.

I'm not telling you to deny your fear or to sweep it under the carpet. I'm not suggesting that you try to minimize the danger or the discomfort of whatever it is you're afraid of. I'm simply suggesting that you think about something else. Throw another film in the projector and watch what happens.

For example, what would you do if you found yourself watching an unpleasant show on TV? You would change the channel, right? You can do exactly the same thing when you find yourself watching an unpleasant show in your mind: you can change the channel and watch something else.

When you're afraid of something, you're picturing what can go wrong. If you want to change the channel, picture what can go right, instead. Instead of picturing the worst thing that can happen, picture the best thing that can happen. Instead of picturing the pain, picture the gain. Instead of picturing what you have to lose, picture what you have to win.

When you change the movie you're watching in your mind, you change your emotional reaction to it. You turn your fear into excitement, your dread into anticipation, your avoidance into action. You can accomplish all of this simply by changing your mental pictures.

Is it really that easy? Yes and no. The movies you're running in your mind are a matter of habit. Changing one of these movies is as difficult, or as easy, as changing any other habit.

You already know how to change your habits. You know how to use visualization, affirmation, pre-memory, and the Thirty-Day Plan. So go ahead and use these tools to teach yourself a new habit, the habit of running a new movie, a movie in which you picture what you have to win instead of what you have to lose. With this new habit, your fear will lose its power over you forever.

*   *   *

Thinking Like a Victim

The second wish killer is to think like a victim. As *Webster's* defines it, a victim is "someone harmed by or suffering from some act, condition, or circumstance."

Do you know anyone who doesn't fit that description? We are all victimized by something—crime, poverty, discrimination, a handicap, a broken home, a lousy boss, fly-away hair. But the only real victim is the person who thinks like one.

Life is a self-service gas station. You can sit in your car and honk, or you can fill the tank yourself. No one honks longer, louder, or with less effect than a victim.

It's easy to think like a victim. For one thing, it feels good. It lets you off the hook. When you're not responsible for what happens to you, you can't be expected to do anything about it. When the cards are stacked against you, you have no choice but to fold, so you never have to face the pressure of playing to win. And you never lack for something to do. You can fill every idle moment with the bittersweet memories of your misfortunes. Unfortunately, you can never fulfill a wish.

When you think like a victim, you turn yourself from a cause into an effect. Nothing will kill a wish faster than that. When you blame the world, you lose your power to change it. In the name of what you can't fix, you sacrifice the things you can fix.

It's not what happens to you that matters in life, it's what you choose to do about it. We are all victims of forces beyond our control. The people who get what they want from life focus on the forces they can control. They choose to live as a cause instead of as an effect.

If you want to be a cause in your own life, don't think like an effect. Instead of worrying about the cards you've been dealt, play them. Instead of asking, "Why me?" ask, *What am I going to do about it?* Instead of feeling sorry for yourself, refuse to settle for less than what you want.

The world owes you only what you are willing to collect. The best way I know to collect is to make your wishes come true.

22 *The Myth of Self-Discipline*

Success flows from passion, not from self-discipline. I'm not suggesting that self-discipline is unimportant. Just the opposite. Self-discipline is the foundation of character, and character is the foundation of all lasting success. The headlines and history books are full of hotshots who fell from grace because they lacked character. Without character, success is meaningless.

But character is only the launching pad—it's not the rocket. The rocket is passion.

Successful people do what they need to do whether they like it or not. That's self-discipline. *Exceptionally* successful people do what they need to do because they love it. That's passion.

If you have to force yourself to make your wish come true, you're working on the wrong wish. Look around you. The people who are wildly successful aren't doing what they hate; they're doing what they love. Or at least they've learned to love what they're doing.

It's easy to fall in love with an effect—we all want to be rich, or famous, or to make a difference in the world—the trick is to fall in love with the cause. The people most likely to become successful, however you measure success, are the ones who fall in love with the processes that cause their success. Fall in love with the cause, and the effect will take care of itself.

When you're in love with the cause, you're following the path of least resistance. Your actions come naturally. You don't have to discipline yourself; you don't have to force yourself; you don't even have to motivate yourself. You simply do what you enjoy doing. The doing then becomes its own reward, and your desired results follow the way dessert follows a great meal.

When you're passionately in love with the process of making your wish come true, you allow yourself to treasure the moment, instead of waiting for some distant payoff. This is what living is all about. The greatest gift you can give yourself is the gift of enjoying today. Why do you think they call it "the present"?

The easiest way to substitute passion for self-discipline is to change the way you think about what you're doing. Instead of asking yourself, "How can I get myself to do this?" ask yourself, *How can I get myself to **enjoy** doing this?* The secret to joy is to find it wherever you look, and to look for it everywhere. Look for it in the tasks that will make your wish come true. Look for it in the doing. Look for it in the challenges you face and the problems you have to solve. Look for it in the moment.

Don't try to talk yourself into feeling this joy; imagine yourself into it instead. Change your mental movie. Enlarge your comfort zone. Instead of running a movie that shows how much you hate what you're doing, run a movie that shows how much you love it. Picture how much you enjoy doing the things that will make your wish come true, and before long you'll enjoy doing them.

At first this new movie might feel uncomfortable, the way you feel when you're trying to acquire any new habit. Just keep practicing until it feels more natural to run the new movie than it does to run the old one.

When you run your new movie, allow yourself to feel the intense emotions you have already connected with your wish. Whatever you deeply feel for your wish, you will soon feel for each step that causes your wish to come true. When you allow yourself to connect positive emotions to every step you take along the way, you will soon find yourself performing every step naturally, without having to discipline yourself to make it happen. No matter what step you're working on, you will feel the emotional satisfaction of working on your entire wish. When you reach that point, causing your wish to come true will seem like the most natural thing in the world, a product of passion and joy, instead of self-discipline.

Play the Pauses

To make music you have to play the pauses, not just the notes. To make a wish, you have to do the same. You have to give yourself moments to relax, to do nothing, to take a breath before moving to the next task.

To persist you must first endure. To endure, you must from time to time allow yourself to recuperate. Nature shows us the way. Summer's frantic growth is offset by the slumber of winter. The violence of a storm relaxes in its aftermath. Creatures great and small labor during the day, and lie up at night. In all that it does, nature builds a balance between exertion and relaxation. We are smart to build that same balance into our own lives.

Even machines take a break. In the life cycle of a machine

there is a balance between operation and maintenance. If you don't maintain the machine—change the oil, recharge the battery, lubricate the moving parts—it will burn itself out. The same is true for people.

People who are successful over the long haul don't allow themselves to burn out. They know how to recuperate. They know how to relax. They know how to play the pauses, along with the notes. They have the discipline to know when to quit.

That's right, quit. When the going gets tough, the tough quit. They take a break. They distance themselves from the situation so they can gain a fresh perspective. They recharge their batteries so they can come back stronger and more effective than ever. You don't read much about this in self-help books. The biographies of great achievers don't dwell on recovery. But at the heart of success, at the core of all achievement, you're always going to find pauses, not just notes.

There is no better example than Winston Churchill. He was a juggernaut—supercharged with energy, ceaselessly active, unstoppable, perhaps the greatest achiever of the twentieth century. How did he do it? He took a nap every day. Even in the darkest months of World War II, when bombs rained nightly on London and hope seemed lost for Britain and perhaps for all of Western civilization, Churchill took his naps. He kept himself going when others would have collapsed. He kept himself going by knowing when to stop.

If you feel stressed, or depressed, or worn out, if you feel ready to give up, the chances are you don't know when to stop. To make your wish come true, you need to pace yourself, not kill yourself. You need to play the pauses.

How you pause is your business. It may be by parachute jumping or rock climbing. It may be by lying in your hammock all afternoon or baking a pie. It may be by watching a movie, or reading a book, or painting a picture. Whatever works for you, do it. Do it often. Build it into your L.A.M.P. Plan. Notes without pauses aren't music, they're just noise.

24 *Follow Through*

Plan Your Finish

I once attended a seminar where one of the exercises called for us to climb a fifty-foot telephone pole, stand on the top, and leap to a trapeze. The object was to learn how to overcome our fears, presumably without killing ourselves (there was a harness to break the fall). Being terrified of heights, I couldn't resist.

To psych myself up to face the challenge, I pictured the process from start to finish as clearly and precisely as if it were already a memory. I ascended the pole; I balanced at the top; I leaped to the trapeze; I practiced the whole thing over and over in my mind before I tried it with my body.

Then I did it, just the way I pictured it. I climbed the pole; I stood on top; I kept my balance in the stiff breeze. And I jumped flawlessly. I sailed through the air and reached for the bar as if I were an Olympic gymnast. Then a curious thing happened. As my body swung out into space fifty feet above the ground, the force of the jump tore my hands from the bar. And I fell.

The harness caught me, just the way it was supposed to do. As the spotters lowered me gently to the ground, all I could think about was how badly I blew it. *I didn't hold on—what went wrong?*

Nothing went wrong. I accomplished exactly what I set out to accomplish, but I hadn't set out to accomplish enough. I never planned my finish.

It never occurred to me that I might need to make a special effort to hold on to the trapeze. I planned the climb. I planned how to keep my balance on the pole. I planned the jump. I planned how I would reach out with perfect form and grab the bar. I just never planned to hold on. I didn't follow through in my mind, so I didn't follow through with my body.

Plan your finish, or your plan is finished.

Finish Your Plan

Sometimes when you're nearing the end of a long and demanding wish, you feel an almost irresistible urge to let down, to relax. Resist it. It's like that warm, cozy feeling you get just before you fall asleep in the snow and freeze to death.

I know I told you to play the pauses, but don't play them when you're beginning the last lap of a race, when you've almost pushed the boulder to the top of the hill, when you're about to make your wish come true. If you relax before the finish, you may never finish. Or you may finish second when you've set your heart on finishing first.

If you feel like relaxing, relax after you've finished and not a moment before. What good is a whodunit one page short of who did it? What good is a boat one plank shy of a bottom? What good is the fastest runner if he never finishes a race, or the ablest politician if he never completes a campaign? What good is the finest surgeon in the world if he never sews you back together?

You get the picture. Finish what you start.

Know What Comes Next

What if the harder you worked, the more likely you were to find yourself out of a job? That's the position you put your subconscious in when you near the end of one wish without having another one in the queue.

When you created your L.A.M.P. Plan, you penciled in your next wish. Part of your follow-through is to begin to focus attention on that wish. Not enough to divert you from your current wish, but enough to let your subconscious mind know there's plenty more work where that came from.

Not that you shouldn't take a break between wishes. Take a week off; take a month off; take a year off. Reward yourself with a vacation. Do whatever you need to do to recharge your power cells. Meanwhile, in the back of your mind, know what comes next.

Anticipate Your Progress

An important part of knowing what comes next is to anticipate your own progress. As you make progress on your wish, your circumstances will change. As your circumstances change, your perspective will change, the way the view changes as you climb a mountain. The higher you go, the more different things look from up there. As your perspective changes, your needs may change. Your objectives may change. Your possibilities may change. Indeed, *you* may change. And the new you may want to change your wish.

Changing your wish may mean revising it to take advantage of your new circumstances, your new perspective, or perhaps some new knowledge or experience you have gained. Or it may mean changing to another wish altogether. This can be a good thing if you change to a better wish. It can be a bad thing if you use it as an excuse to quit.

Completing a wish, in itself, has value. One of the most useful habits you will ever develop is to finish what you start. But sometimes you outgrow your objective before you reach it. To mix metaphors, the fine line you walk is in deciding when to change horses in the middle of the stream, and when not to. If you have a tendency to change wishes too quickly, you may never complete a wish. For that matter, you may never complete anything. But if you wait too long to make a needed change, and end up completing a wish that no longer has value for you, you may waste time that could be put to much better use working on another wish.

A vital part of managing your progress is to deal with the changes and the challenges your progress brings. For example, suppose your wish is to achieve financial independence. As you make progress on your wish, you make more money. As you make more money, the world begins to treat you differently. Even your friends don't look at you quite the same way. Perhaps you change, or perhaps others simply change toward you. Whatever the reasons for these changes, if you perceive them to be unpleasant, you may begin to sabotage your own progress. Unless you are prepared to adjust to the changes that come as a result of your success.

Another problem that may surface as you begin to accumulate wealth is that you may begin to realize that you need more than wealth to get where you want to go. Perhaps you need more of a sense of accomplishment, or fulfillment, or love, none of which money can buy. Your original wish is no longer enough for you, so you need to change that wish accordingly.

Another variation on this same wish is that as you make progress, you begin to realize that you can accumulate a great deal more wealth than you had ever imagined. Rich people say that earning that first million dollars is the hardest. What they mean is that once you've earned a million dollars, things look different. Your view is different from up there. Your contacts are different. You are different. You know how to make money, and the possibilities this opens to you are much greater than they were when you began your journey. This change in perspective may call for you to adjust your wish.

Successful follow-through means that you plan not just for the wish, but for the changes caused by making progress on that wish. And you retain the flexibility not just to stay the course, but to change course when it makes sense to do so.

25 *Patience*

In one way or another, almost everything I've ever done wrong in my life has been the result of giving in to the urge for instant gratification. The "I want it now" syndrome has caused me more grief than anything else I can think of.

Perhaps you have noticed a similar trend in your life. Have you ever followed the urge to get rich quickly, and then lost your shirt? Have you ever chosen to go to a party instead of completing a work assignment that was due the next day? Have you ever bought something on credit because you couldn't wait long enough to pay cash, and then found your bills mounting to the point where you seemed to be paying more for interest than you were for rent? If you've done any of these things, then you know what I'm talking about.

I once heard "shortcut" defined as the longest distance between two points. That's a great way to describe instant gratification. It's a lot harder to get rich quickly than it is to get rich slowly. It's a lot harder to catch up on your work once you've let yourself fall behind than it is to simply do what you're supposed to do when you're supposed to do it. It's a lot harder to become financially independent when you're paying interest to a bank for your credit card, than it is when that same bank is paying you interest for putting money into a savings account.

But despite the suffering that is bound to come from it, the urge to gratify an immediate desire is often so strong that we tend to forget the pain it will cause us in the end. We insist on living in our dream house today, even though we know it will cost us three times what it's worth in interest. We insist on eating our favorite foods today, even though we know we'll have to spend the rest of our lives on a diet. We insist on goofing off today, even though we know we're sentencing ourselves to working that much harder tomorrow.

If you want to make your wishes come true, sooner or later you're going to have to come to grips with the desire for instant gratification. The cornerstone for making a successful wish is the willingness to pay the price to make that wish come true. Part of that price is paid in terms of sacrifice. And sacrifice means giving up the pleasures of instant gratification when those pleasures interfere with your wish.

Patience

It may be the world's oldest cliché, but patience really is a virtue. Our greatest achievements are accomplished over time, with considerable dedication and perseverance. Neither of these qualities would be possible without patience. "Everything comes to him who waits," as the old saying goes. The secret to waiting is patience.

But as a culture, we are more likely to act as if impatience is a virtue. How often have you heard someone proclaim "I have no patience!" as if he were proud of his shortcoming? How often do you see people wear their impatience as if it were a badge of honor? Yet impatience is just another word for instant gratification. And nothing could be more wrongheaded than to glorify instant gratification. Nothing could be more destructive of happiness, fulfillment, and success. Nothing could be more ruinous for a wish.

As much as we rant and rave about the evils of instant gratification, as devoutly as we moralize against it, as fervently as we condemn it, the only thing that really matters is to find a cure. Ironically, the cure is right in front of us. It's been there all along. In the battle against instant gratification, the most potent weapon of all is patience.

Patience is the ability to wait for an outcome, instead of insisting on having that outcome at once. Patience is the ability to bide your time while all the forces that you cannot control align themselves to help you accomplish what you cannot do alone. If we really want to cure the affliction called instant gratification, all we need do is develop patience. But how?

We can start by realizing that patience is not just a virtue, it's a skill. Moreover, it's a learnable skill, a skill that can be mastered by anyone. And patience is one of life's most enjoyable skills because it allows you to relax, to regain your self-control, to restore a sense of well-being and balance—even in the midst of chaos.

Patience allows you to rise above the turmoil and confusion of a hectic life and understand that there are forces at work far beyond what you alone can master. If you're willing to wait for these forces—in other words, if you're patient—they can be made to work for you, instead of against you.

But how do you learn patience? The same way you learned every other skill you now possess: through practice. Specifically, you practice waiting.

The next time you have to wait for something, think of it as practice. Think of it not as a waste of time but as a way to use time to your advantage. Think of it as if you've been given a chance to develop a skill that, once mastered, will bring you the kind of joy and peace of mind that otherwise you could only dream about.

Once you embrace patience as a source of strength in making your wishes come true, and you embrace waiting as a way to develop that strength, then delays will only encourage you, setbacks will only strengthen you, and time—perhaps for the first time in your life—will finally be on your side.

26 *Wake Up*

Other animals spend their lives locked in a cycle of instinct. When they're hungry, they eat. When they're frightened, they run. When they come into season, they mate. When they're angry, they fight. They live the way their genes and their environment have programmed them to live because they have no choice. But we do.

We, too, are programmed by our genes and by our environment. But we can transcend our programming. We have been given the awesome power not just to respond to what the world throws at us, but to choose our response. We can literally program ourselves.

Alone among the animals, we have been given what it takes to make our lives serve our own ends instead of the ends that have been handed down to us. We can break the chain of events that has shaped us and learn to shape ourselves. We have been given the extraordinary power to participate in our own fate.

And not one in ten of us knows it.

Like the elephant, we are unconscious of our own strength. When it comes to understanding the incredible power we have to make a difference in our own lives, we might as well be asleep.

Choice

What is the secret to this incredible power? Other animals live the way they are programmed to live because they literally have no choice—they are controlled by the process of stimulus and response. But for human beings there is a little gap between stimulus and response. It is in this gap that we have the power to exercise the characteristic that is most truly human: the power to choose.

The power to choose lies at the heart of every human success, every human achievement, and every human failure. This is the power that gives us the ability—and the obligation—to make of our lives whatever we will.

We can wield this power consciously, deliberately, and intentionally, or we can pretend it doesn't exist. We can pretend we have no choice. But we can only pretend, because we can no more escape our obligation to choose than we can escape our obligation to breathe. Even when we refuse to choose, we are making the choice to refuse.

Whether you like it or not, you are going to have to make choices in your life. Your circumstances will never force you to act; they will force you merely to choose. And it will be your choices, not your circumstances, that will make you whoever you become. You might not like your choices. You might not like having to choose. But in the end, choose you must and choose you will. You will choose the kind of person you want to be, and the kind of life you want to live. The point of learning how to wish is simply to make your choices work for you, instead of against you.

So if you want to make your wishes come true, wake up to this little gap between stimulus and response. Wake up to the power you have to make choices. Not the choices that have been handed down to you by society, or by your family, or by your job, but the choices that you in your heart of hearts want to make for yourself. If you really want to make your wishes come true, wake up to your own strength. Wake up to the role you play in your own destiny. Wake up to the power you have to choose what you think, do, and say.

The moment you understand that your life is whatever you make of it by choice, you will awaken to an astonishing new world. Like an elephant who suddenly discovers he's the biggest, baddest animal in the jungle, you will become aware of the limitless possibilities that surround you. You will feel at once a sense of great humility and great power; humility because all of life is a gift; and power because you have been given the most potent gift of all—the power to choose.

But to make the most of this power, you must awake. To wake up is to grow up. As children, we are by nature dependent. Too often, as adults, we choose to remain dependent. We rely on others, or on circumstances, to give us what we want, instead of taking that responsibility upon ourselves. But once you awaken to the power of choice, once you become aware of your own strength, you become forever independent. Once you realize that you can give yourself whatever you want, you are no longer content to settle for less.

Waking up is like coming to your senses. You see things more clearly than ever before. You feel a greater sense of freedom, a greater sense of possibility. Your limitations are limitations no more. You see them for what they really are—bad dreams. And then they quickly lose their power over you, the way a nightmare loses its edge the moment you awaken. You find yourself free to imagine more useful thoughts, to dream more pleasant dreams, and to turn those dreams into reality.

The difference between being asleep and being awake is the difference between having a dream and making that dream come true. That is what happens when you're awake. That is the kind of gift you can give yourself when you know your own strength. That is the kind of life you can lead when you understand your power to choose, and choose to use it.

Conclusion

The time has come for me to ask you a question. This is one of the most important questions I know. It is also one of the most powerful questions I know. It is a question that has the potential to change your life from this moment on.

Now that you know your own strength; now that you know about the magic lamp that you were given at birth; now that you know how to make your own wishes come true; what are you going to do about it?

Are you going to make your wishes come true, or are you going to settle for something less? Are you going to turn the L.A.M.P. Process into a habit that can bring you literally anything you want for the rest of your life? Or are you going to let the next ten years pass the way the last ten did? There is nothing wrong with that, as long as you don't mind being in the same place ten years from now that you are today.

If you want to make your wishes come true, you have a decision to make. You have to decide whether you want to be a cause or an effect. You have to decide whether you want to be a hammer or a nail. You have to decide whether, when you put this book down, you are willing to set in motion the causes of whatever effects you desire.

The choice is up to you. With all my heart I would love to be able to reach out and flip a little switch in your brain that would activate your magic lamp and supercharge you with enough energy to make your wishes come true for the rest of your life. But I can't do that. Only you can flip that switch. Only you can make that one choice that makes everything else possible. The best I can do is to offer this parting thought:

Wishing really works, if you do.

Lend a Copy to a Friend

There is nothing more useless than a book sitting on a bookshelf; there is nothing more powerful than the same book in the hands of someone who can use it. If you think *The Magic Lamp* is worth reading, please lend your copy to a friend. Pass it around. Wear it out. Let others benefit from your investment the way you have.

Success Stories

Would you like to have your success story published in the next edition of *The Magic Lamp?* Send an e-mail describing your wish and telling how *The Magic Lamp* helped you make it come true. If your story is selected for publication, you will receive a copy of the next edition, signed by the author, and complete with a new chapter full of success stories—including your own. E-mail: LAMP@selfhelp.com

Frequently Asked Questions About Making Your Wishes Come True

What is the difference between wishing and goal setting?

Wishing is goal setting, but it is goal setting with snap crackle and pop. Goals can take you anywhere you want to go, but they rarely give you the inspiration you need to get there. Wishing is different. Wishing has impact—like being struck by lightning instead of by a lightning bug. Wishing gives you the freedom to dream, and then it gives you the inspiration you need to make your dreams come true. Wishing provides the emotional spark that can set your life ablaze with success.

Why don't more people set goals?

We all set goals, but most of us don't realize it. Every time you plan a vacation and then take it, you're setting (and achieving) a goal. Every time you decide you want to buy something, look for what you want, shop around for the best price, and then buy it, you're setting (and achieving) a goal. Every time you create a shopping list, visit the grocery store, find the items you're looking for, and bring them home, you're setting (and achieving) a goal.

Most of us don't realize that the same process that enables us to obtain what we want from the supermarket can also let us obtain the career we want. Most of us don't realize that the same process that enables us to go out and buy a new television also enables us to have the house we want, and the income we want, and the relationships we want. Most of us don't realize that the same process that enables us to take a successful vacation also enables us to live a successful life. The difference between successful people and unsuccessful people isn't whether or not they set goals, but whether or not they *consciously* set goals, and understand the power of setting goals.

What if I don't know what to wish for?

Then your first wish should be to figure out what you want to wish for. That is as valid as any other wish on the planet, and it will make all of your other wishes possible. The secret is to make it a formal wish. Take it through the entire L.A.M.P. Process. Make it presentable. Create a L.A.M.P. Plan for it. Put your plan into action. Keep working your L.A.M.P. Plan until you have made your wish come true. At that point you will have successfully completed your first wish—you'll know what to wish for— and you'll have your second wish ready to go.

*   *   *

How many wishes should I work on at once?

The short answer is as many as you can handle. An even shorter answer is "one." Wishing is hard work. If you make it too hard, you'll soon find other ways to spend your time. When people ask me how many wishes I work on at the same time, I tell them two: one for home and one for work. Many people find that hard to believe. I remember a young man at one of my seminars who told me he had at least fifty wishes he was working on at any one time. Gently, I tried to explain that he didn't understand what I meant by wishing. Wishing means creating a L.A.M.P. Plan. Wishing means making your wish presentable. Wishing means making progress reports. Try that with fifty wishes at a time and you'll run screaming from the room.

When I say that I work on two wishes at a time, I mean that I work through two complete L.A.M.P. Processes at a time. I go all out for two different wishes. Typically, they are big wishes, important wishes. By working on them, other things in my life just seem to fall into place around them. The discipline of working seriously on two wishes—or even a single wish—affects everything else I do. It tends to make me more organized and result oriented in everything I happen to be working on, whether it's part of my formal wish or not.

What is the difference between a wish and a prayer?

A prayer is when you ask for something from your god. A wish is when you ask for something from yourself.

I tried the L.A.M.P. Process and it didn't work. What do I do now?

The L.A.M.P. Process says that you have to *L*ock on, *A*ct, *M*anage your progress, and *P*ersist until you get what you want. By definition, you can't say, "It doesn't work"; you can say only that "I gave up before it had a chance to work." In other words, you didn't persist until you got what you wanted.

The L.A.M.P Process always works. It works because it is based on one of the fundamental building blocks of the universe: the law of cause and effect. If you set in motion the appropriate cause, the effect will take care of itself. Period. End of discussion. If the effect is missing—in other words, if you aren't getting what you want from life—then you can be certain you have yet to set in motion the appropriate cause. You can be equally certain that once you set that cause in motion, the effect will follow. The L.A.M.P Process can't fail any more than the law of cause and effect can fail, because the L.A.M.P Process is a strategy for employing the law of cause and effect to your advantage.

If you aren't yet getting the results you want, then you aren't yet doing everything you need to do to make your wish come true. For example, you may not have made your wish entirely presentable. Or perhaps you haven't given yourself enough time. Or your plan may not take you where you want to go.

This last problem is one of the most common. For example, suppose you asked a friend for directions to a particular destination, and he told you to take a right, the next two lefts, and then keep walking until you get there. If his directions are wrong, then you will never reach your destination. You just can't get there from here. But if his directions are right, you have to keep going until you reach your destination. Imagine the reception you would get from your friend if you called him up midway and said, "Your directions aren't working." He would laugh at you, the way a parent laughs at an impatient child, and say, "You've given up too soon. You have to keep going until you get there."

The same is true for the L.A.M.P. Process. If your plan will take you where you want to go, then you have to keep going until you get there. But if your plan will not take you where you want to go, then no matter how hard you work, you'll never get there. If you're not getting the results you want, don't abandon the process. Create a plan that works and keep working it until you make your wish come true.

How can I tell when my plan won't take me where I want to go?

Your first clue is when you notice your plan is not working. It may be that the plan itself is at fault. Or it may be that you are not working it properly. Or it may be that it takes longer than you think to complete your plan. Or the plan may be working fine, but you haven't created the appropriate milestones and progress reports, so you can't tell. (You can be winning but never know it because you aren't keeping score.)

Rather than waiting for a plan to fail and prove itself to be a bad plan, I suggest you evaluate it before you start working the plan, and then reevaluate it at regular intervals. Ask questions like these: Will the steps you've outlined, properly executed, take you where you want to go? Have you given yourself enough time to learn the necessary skills and perform the necessary tasks as outlined in your plan? Do you have enough money and enough help to complete your plan? Are you intimidated by any of the steps? (If so, you'll never get past them.) If, after examining your plan, you're convinced that it will work, then you have only to complete it successfully to make your wish come true.

How do I motivate myself to work on my wishes?

Why do people worry so much about motivation? Either you have it, or you don't. You can't create motivation—unless you are motivated to do so. And that's the point. Either you are motivated, or you're not. If you're not, why worry about it?

Not to put too fine a point on it, but if you aren't motivated, then you don't care enough to act. If you don't care enough to act, then why worry about it? Why put yourself through all that worry and angst when you have no intention of doing anything about it? Better simply to accept who you are and get on with it.

Better to get on with your life than to live it in shades of gray, where you're unhappy, but not unhappy enough to do anything about it. That's like being hungry, but not hungry enough to feed yourself. Or being thirsty, but not thirsty enough to take a drink. Or being cold, but not cold enough to put on a coat. All in all, not a pleasant frame of mind.

Think of it this way, if you're unhappy with your life but you're not willing to do anything about it, then you're probably not as unhappy as you think. For people to make changes in their lives, they need to reach a threshold at which their dissatisfaction becomes greater than their resistance to change. Once they reach that threshold, they will act. But until they reach it, they will not act. They will remain unmotivated because they do not have sufficient reason to change.

And that brings us to the crux of the issue. If you aren't motivated to do something, that simply means you don't have a compelling enough reason to do it. So don't worry about changing your ways, worry about changing your reasons. Give yourself a compelling enough reason to do something, and you'll find it the most natural thing in the world to do.

When you say wishing can give you anything you want, you don't literally mean "anything," do you?

Yes, I mean *anything*. Many people refuse to believe that they can have anything they want from life. They are so deeply conditioned to think in terms of limitations that they never think in terms of possibilities. They never allow themselves to dream.

Wishing gives you the freedom to dream. And then it gives you the power to make your dreams come true. But you must fulfill these three requirements:

1. You must be willing to pay the price to get what you want.
2. You must be willing to persist until you get what you want.
3. What you want must be humanly possible.

That last requirement is the excuse that people most often use to fail. They tell themselves that something is impossible, so they don't bother to try. Or if they do try, and they don't get what they want, they assume that it must be impossible. They let their results determine their beliefs, instead of letting their beliefs determine their results.

If you want to make things happen in your life, assume that a wish is possible until proven otherwise. And remember that you can never prove otherwise. You can give up, but you can't prove that something is impossible. You can prove that what you've attempted to do hasn't worked, but you can't prove that it will never work.

On the other hand, if you think something is impossible, you make it impossible for you. Sometimes the whole world does this. Consider the four-minute mile. Until the middle of the twentieth century, the experts said it was impossible for human beings to run faster than a four-minute mile. Decade after decade the finest runners in the world proved them right. Until 1954, when Roger Bannister broke the four-minute barrier. Within months after he accomplished this "humanly impossible" feat, several other runners managed to do the same thing. They no longer believed it to be impossible, so it no longer was.

I know that I have to make some changes in my life, but it's not easy. How do I get myself to change?

The answer is so simple that you probably won't believe it: to make changes in your life, make changes in your habits.

You do what you do because you're used to it. To change what you're doing, get used to doing something else. An entire chapter of *The Magic Lamp* is devoted to changing habits (see chapter 7), but for now, take this to heart: You can change any habit the same way you created it in the first place—through practice and repetition. To create any new behavior, practice it enough until it becomes a habit.

Now let's talk about part two of this answer. As human beings, we do what we do because it feels good. But all too often what feels good isn't good for us (smoking, overeating, etc.). We think in terms of short-term pleasure, instead of long-term benefit. To change this natural tendency, change your outlook. Instead of doing what *feels* good, start doing what *is* good, even when it doesn't feel so good. Instead of making decisions based on what mood you're in, make them based on what is important to you. Instead of thinking only of what you feel like doing, think of the consequences of your actions. Will they produce the long-term results you desire? Or will they set you back? In the end, you'll still have to change your habits, but knowing why you're doing it and how you'll benefit from it will make those changes easier to swallow.

Much of what I do is self-destructive. How do I change that?

As human beings, it's the most natural thing in the world for us to want to do what we feel like doing. But a lot of what we may feel like doing can be self-destructive (such as smoking, drinking, losing our temper, overeating, partying all night, etc.). Sometimes these self-destructive behaviors are a symptom of a psychological problem, one for which we should seek professional help. More often our self-destructive tendencies are habits that we learned before we knew enough to understand how undesirable these habits were.

And therein lies the cure. If a self-destructive action is a habit we formed before we knew better, then the way to change that habit is to know better. Think about what you're doing, instead of simply doing it. Think about the consequences of your act, and decide if those consequences are worth it. If they are worth it, then you're never going to change. But if they aren't, then act on that information. Act as if you really do know better. Act as if you really are taking into account the long-term consequences of your actions. If this new perspective suggests that you need to make a change in something you do, then make that change. If you have to break an old habit, then break it—by creating a new habit. You already know how to create new habits, from chapter 7 of this book. Once you get your habits under control, you'll find that everything else will fall into place.

Why do I keep doing things that set me back instead of moving me forward?

My theory of success is simple: whatever you want from life, if you set in motion the appropriate cause, the effect will take care of itself. This is called the law of cause and effect, and it applies to human behavior the same way it applies to everything else in nature.

People who are successful tend to use this law to their advantage. People who are not successful tend to ignore this law, or are ignorant of it altogether.

Nothing is more perplexing to me than to see how many people think they can violate this law with impunity. A case in point is people who smoke cigarettes. Mountains of evidence proves that smoking *causes* both heart disease and lung cancer. Even the tobacco companies are finally willing to admit it. But millions of people smoke nevertheless, as if they think that the negative effects of smoking will somehow not apply to them. It's as if these people think they are above the law of cause and effect.

But it's not just smokers who ignore the law of cause and effect. From time to time, we all do. We all do things we know are not good for us, and then we hope we'll get away with them. But we never do. We may never notice the relationship between the cause and the effect (consider the person who always seems to hate his employer, but can't figure out why it's so hard to hold a job). Or we may misunderstand the cause (consider the smoker who holds a tobacco company responsible for his lung cancer, instead of holding himself responsible for smoking). Either way, we cannot escape the results of our own actions, even though we may not understand how those actions ultimately cause our results.

In the end, it all boils down to this: The people who are unsuccessful in life are the ones who habitually set in motion the causes of effects that they don't want. The people who are successful in life are the ones who habitually set in motion the causes of effects that they do want.

If you find yourself taking two steps back for every one step forward, think about the causes you're setting in motion. Think about where those causes will take you. Think about how you behave in any given situation, and how that behavior might be doing you in.

For example, think about your eating habits, and what they might be doing to your body, your health, and your level of energy. Think about your work habits and what they might be doing to your chances for advancement. Think about the way you relate to other people, and what those habits might be doing to your relationships. In each instance, the question you need to answer is this: If I keep doing what I'm doing right now, am I likely to get the results I want? If the answer is no, then you're going to need to set in motion some different causes.

This isn't rocket science. It isn't about motivation, determination, positive thinking, or any of the other magic bullets that are pedaled so energetically by the self-improvement industry. Success is simply a matter of cause and effect.

If you want to know whether or not you're successful, take a look at your life and ask yourself: Am I setting in motion the causes of whatever effects I desire? If the answer is *yes,* then you have only to keep on your present course, and the effects will take care of themselves. But if the answer is *no,* then you have a useful clue about why things don't seem to be going your way. More important, now you know what to do about it. You know you have to identify what will cause the effects you want, and then set those causes in motion.

How do I get myself to follow through on my wishes?

In a word, *focus.* Sometimes it seems as if life is a conspiracy to distract us from what we really want to do. This is no illusion. Our lives are subject to a natural principle called entropy, a term borrowed from the science of thermodynamics. Entropy means that the natural world tends to decay. Ice melts. Stars light the heavens for billions of years, then burn out. Mountains crumble to the sea. Human beings grow old and die.

Entropy also applies to our thoughts and actions. We spend five years learning French, and five years later we've forgotten it. A wealthy man dies, leaving a fortune to his heirs, and in a generation they are paupers. We approach a major project, full of enthusiasm and motivation, and before we know it we are busy doing something else and the project grinds to a halt. We have an entire week at home to get some real work done, and we end up puttering our time away on a dozen unimportant tasks.

All of these are examples of entropy at work. And all are the norm, rather than the exception. The natural thing for us to do is to putter away our days taking care of all the petty details that life seems only too happy to throw our way. But that's not the way to make our wishes come true.

The opposite of entropy is focus. Instead of letting our time, and energy, and resources slip away, focus means we put them to good use—our use—instead of ceding them to every distraction that happens by. Perhaps that is why success is so rare, compared to the number of people who claim to be interested in succeeding. Few of us ever learn how to fight entropy; in fact, few of us know we're at war—at war with the natural tendency to allow our precious time and energy to dissipate. But that is precisely why it is so hard to learn something, to build something, to grow something. Because entropy makes it hard. Entropy tugs at us every step of the way, making it easier to forget than it is to learn, easier to destroy than it is to build, easier to kill than it is to grow.

Life is a struggle against entropy, a struggle against the forces of decay. We are struggling against a universe that takes it for granted that everything, in its time, shall pass—including us, and everything we try to do.

Once we understand this, once we know what we're dealing with, we can devote our lives to focus and to growth—the opposites of entropy—and begin to make our wishes come true.

No sooner do I make a wish then I forget about it. How can I keep myself focused on my wish?

Keep your wish in front of you. There are a number of ways to do this, all of which are discussed in chapter 13 of *The Magic Lamp*. In a nutshell, anything you do to expose yourself to your wish several times each day will help you stay focused on making that wish come true. For example, you can write your wish on a Post-it note and stick it on your bathroom mirror. You can ask your friends to call you each day and remind you of your wish. You can send yourself an e-mail message several times a day—automatically—reminding you of your wish. The more you keep your wish in front of you, the more likely you are to make it come true.

I'm afraid to set goals—what you call wishes— because I don't want to turn into a driven person.

I can't help wonder what you mean by "driven." If you mean that you work so hard you never smell the roses, then I would say that's a pretty bleak existence, and I wouldn't want any part of it, either. But if by "driven" you mean the act of passionately following something that gives you great joy, I would hate to miss out on that. So would you, I suspect.

What if being driven meant that you found the very thing that so many human beings lack: a purpose? What if being driven simply meant that you were driven to fulfill this purpose? And what if fulfilling this purpose filled your life with great meaning and joy? Would that be such a tough way to live?

When people say that they don't want to be "driven," I suspect they mean that they don't want to have their nose so close to the grindstone that they miss the world around them. And they are right. But look at this from another perspective. You can be driven to get the most out of life. You can be driven to fulfill your purpose. You can be driven to fill your life with meaning. In this case, being driven is a good thing. So good that you might want to give it a try.

From now on, don't think of wishing as something that makes you driven, think of it as something that gives you a sense of direction, a sense of something worth working for. And think of a wish not as something that drives you, but as something that guides you—precisely where you want to go.

I keep making wishes and I keep being disappointed. Everything disappoints me: my family, my friends, my job. What can I do about it?

There is no better prescription for unhappiness than to keep track of what you're not getting from life. And there is no better prescription for happiness than to bend your time, your energy, and your talent toward what you give to the world, instead of what you get.

No doubt you have heard that it is more blessed to give than to receive. That's not just a moral principle, it's a profound psychological insight. Giving is more fulfilling than receiving. Giving is more rewarding than receiving. Giving is just more fun.

Receiving rarely reaches the part of us that needs to be touched by others. But giving does, by letting us touch the lives of others. Giving makes us whole. Giving makes us human. If you want to figure out how to find success and happiness in your life, the prescription is simple: stop focusing on what you can take from the world, and start focusing on what you can give.

Don't goals take the spontaneity out of life?

It depends what you mean by spontaneity. Are we talking about spontaneous anxiety? Spontaneous hopelessness? Spontaneous aimlessness? Spontaneous frustration? Those are the states of mind that most often accompany the purely spontaneous existence of someone who lives life without a direction, without a purpose, without a mission.

It's easy to think of goals as chores that squeeze all the juice from life and leave nothing but the rind. I wanted to put a different spin on goals, which is why I wrote *The Magic Lamp*. I wanted the reader to think of goals as if they were as exciting and inspiring as wishes in a fairy tale, because they can be if you allow yourself to think that way. They can be if you accept yourself as just naturally a goal-directed creature, and then learn how to harness your natural, goal-setting powers.

Once you begin to think in terms of wishes, then you can begin to appreciate what goals are meant to be: an intimate and emotionally charged expression of what you want most from life. Goals provide meaning and purpose to our everyday existence, without which our lives would be as empty as the ocean without water. A well formed goal—a wish—doesn't drain you of emotion, it fills you with emotion. It inspires you. It gives you a reason to jump out of bed in the morning. It fills your days with meaning, because you fill them with meaningful work. Far from removing the spontaneity from life, a well-formed wish provides precisely the backdrop of purpose against which spontaneity can be most appreciated and enjoyed.

How do I get started?

Figure out what you want. That's where everything starts. Once you know what you want, everything else falls into place. Then you simply take out a pad of paper and make a list of the things you need to do to get what you want. List what you have to do, what you have to learn, whom you have to meet, and everything else you need to do to make your wish come true.

Next, organize your list in order of what comes first. Whenever you find a step that is so large it intimidates you, break it into smaller, less daunting steps, until you have a complete plan of all the steps you need to take to get from where you are to where you want to be.

At that point, all you have to do is to start working your plan. It makes sense to start at the beginning, of course, but you don't have to start there. You can start on the middle step, or at the end. The important thing is to start. Once you take action, you become a body in motion. Once you become a body in motion, you'll tend to stay in motion, one step after another, until before you know it you've made your wish come true.

I understand the value of setting goals; I understand the value of wishing. But how do I get myself to just do it?

You've answered your own question: *Just do it.* Don't think about it. Don't worry about it. Don't theorize about it. Just do it. Between those who just do it and those who just don't is a chasm that separates the successful people from the unsuccessful. General George Patton once said that a mediocre plan, violently executed, is more effective than a perfect plan that is executed half-heartedly. The key to success is to take action. The action doesn't have to be perfect. The timing doesn't have to be perfect. The plan doesn't have to be perfect. But you do have to act. The difference between those who do and those who don't is the difference between those who win and those who lose, between those who succeed and those who fail, between those who live the good life and those who only dream about it.

How can I make my wishes come true if I don't possess any talent to speak of?

Don't worry about talent, worry about desire. Success is much more often a result of desire than it is of talent.

Consider Michael Jordan. One would assume that he was born with the talent to become the world's greatest basketball player. But if that were true, why did he get cut from his high school basketball team? And why did he become so much better a player than did millions of other young men who were not cut from their high school basketball teams?

Michael's secret isn't his talent; it's his heart and his head. Michael wants to win, as much as anyone who has ever played the game. He will accept no less from himself. He will accept no less from his teammates. He created his talent for basketball based on his will to excel. And then he made the most of it.

Of course, you could argue that Michael was given the height to play basketball. But many men are given such height, and how many of them have ever played the game the way he does? You could argue that Michael was given tremendous leaping ability and great speed. But there are other men who can jump at least as high and move at least as quickly. Why don't they play the way Michael does?

The answer to all these questions is this: Don't get hung up on how tall someone is, or how fast, how strong, or how talented. Those are nice talents to have, but more important than all of them put together is desire. If you *want* to be faster, you can be. If you *want* to be stronger, you can be. If you *want* to be taller, well, I guess there isn't much you can do about your height—

except to ignore it. That's what Spud Webb did. He was only five feet seven inches tall—nearly a foot shorter than Michael Jordan—but Spud still managed to win the Slam Dunk contest in the NBA.

This isn't about sports. It's about living. It's about a principle that applies to everything you do. The principle is this: Don't look to your talent to make yourself successful; look to your desire. Keep in mind the story of the heavyweight boxer who was making his way through a crowd of spectators after losing a fight. A short man pressed forward and yelled, "You wimp! If I were as big as you are, I would be the heavyweight champion of the world." The heavyweight turned to the smaller man and said, "Then why aren't you the lightweight champion of the world?"

The race doesn't go to the swiftest; it goes to the one who refuses to lose.

What do I do about my wish when I feel discouraged?

Feeling discouraged is a matter of belief. Either you believe you can make your wish come true or you don't. If you don't, then drop what you're doing and start working on a wish that you do believe in. If you do believe that your wish will succeed, then why waste time feeling discouraged? You're just lying to yourself. You're telling yourself to worry when you know perfectly well you have nothing to worry about.

The other way to deal with discouragement is to recognize it for what it is: a mood—a *bad* mood. Like all moods, it will pass. Keep working, keep moving forward on your wish regardless of how you feel, and before you know it, your discouragement will have vanished, and in its place you'll find a sense of accomplishment from all the progress you have made.

As hard as I try to avoid them, I keep making mistakes. What can I do about this?

Check your pulse. If you still have one, then you're going to make mistakes. That's the joy of being human.

There are two kinds of mistakes, the accidental ones, and the ones we make on purpose. You can't avoid the accidental ones. So don't worry about them. Learn from them. Keep in mind that good judgment is the result of experience, and experience is the result of bad judgment.

The more dangerous mistakes are the ones we make on purpose. It may seem strange to suggest that we make mistakes on purpose, but we do. Overeating is an example of a mistake we knowingly commit. Smoking is another. Anything we do when we know full well that it isn't good for us is an intentional mistake. Anything we do that accomplishes the opposite of what we intend—and yet we do it anyway—is an intentional mistake. In both cases, we do our best to ignore the law of cause and effect. The problem is, the law of cause and effect won't ignore us.

If you want to make your wishes come true, you must understand that the law of cause and effect cannot be suspended; it cannot be delayed; it cannot be repealed. Successful wishing is about setting in motion causes that take you where you want to go. Intentional mistakes set in motion causes that take you in the opposite direction. If you want to make the most of your time and your energy and your talent, take the law of cause and effect as seriously as it takes you. Think of the consequences of your actions, and act accordingly. Think of the causes you set in motion and whether they will bring you the effects you desire. Act as if everything you do makes a difference in the quality of your life, because it does. Set in motion the causes that will make your wishes come true, and avoid the causes—the deliberate mistakes—that bring you the things in life you would rather avoid.

Doesn't success have to be painful?

Quite the opposite. When people talk about success, they inevitably talk about hard work. And for good reason: success requires hard work. But what is not spoken of as often, though it is at the heart of the matter, is joy. Success doesn't have to be painful, any more than hard work has to be painful.

Have you ever studied the face of someone who is deeply involved in a task? You are far more likely to find an expression of joy, or at least of utter absorption, than you are to find a look of pain. People who wear a pained expression while they are working are the ones who are not absorbed in what they are doing. They are thinking about what else they might be doing. They are thinking about what they are missing. They are thinking about how much they dislike their work. Their pain is inflicted not by their attention to their work, but by their lack of it.

There are many millions of people who grind through one week after another engaged in such "work." But it is not what they are doing that is hard on them, it is what they are not doing. It is the frame of mind with which they relate to their work that causes them to suffer. And it's a frame of mind that is foreign to people who are truly successful.

These people have found the true secret to getting what they want from life: they allow themselves to enjoy the process. They allow themselves to become absorbed in the process. They are deeply engaged in whatever it is they are doing, and they enjoy the process as much as they enjoy the results.

True success is far more likely to be joyful than to be painful, because it is far more likely to be the result of doing what you enjoy, than of doing what causes you pain.

I keep working on my wish over time, but I never seem to get anywhere. How can I get off dead center and move forward?

There are two kinds of wishes. The first I call a *progressive wish*. This kind of wish keeps moving forward. With every step you take, you move closer to making your wish come true. Writing a book is a progressive wish, or building a house, or learning to play a musical instrument. Whatever you accomplish one day will be there to build on the next.

The second kind of wish I call a *regressive wish*. With this kind of wish, you can move one step forward today, and then if you aren't careful you can slide two steps backward tomorrow. Dieting is a regressive wish, because it is so easy to go on an eating binge over a single weekend and ruin everything you've accomplished during the prior month. Saving money is another example of a regressive wish: a single spending spree can wipe out a year of savings. Relationships are also in this category, because a slip of the tongue or an inappropriate action can set a relationship back to the beginning—or worse.

The important thing to remember about regressive wishes is that they require more than time to make them work. They also require consistent effort. For example, you can diet for five years and never lose a pound if for every pound you lose you gain back two.

In chapter 9, Ellis's Law states the following: *Even ordinary effort, over time, yields extraordinary results.* But when you're dealing with a regressive wish you have to modify this law, as follows: *Even ordinary effort—if consistent—over time will yield extraordinary results.*

The most effective way I know to deal with a regressive wish is to take it one day at a time. Don't worry about tomorrow, or next week. Just get through today. Do what you're supposed to do today, and after enough "todays," tomorrow will shape up just fine.

The other piece of the puzzle is to tell yourself that with a regressive wish you are going to have to start all over again whenever you fall off the wagon. One slip and back you go to the beginning. The idea is to make the penalty so high for falling off the wagon, that you choose to stay on the wagon. This is how recovering alcoholics regain control over their lives. They know that if they ever again touch even a drop of alcohol, they will have to begin the whole, painful process of recovery all over again. That's one heck of a price to pay. The price is so high that it's not worth the risk to take a step backward, even once.

There is method to this madness. Alcoholics can tell you to the day how long it has been since their last drink. They use the accumulating time to their advantage, because it makes their stake in maintaining their success ever larger, with every passing day. With every day they have more to lose, so every day gives them one more reason to succeed.

The idea is to place inertia on your side. The more days you move forward, the more momentum there is for you to keep moving forward. The longer the unbroken string of days you have spent doing the right thing, the less your chance of doing the wrong thing. Inertia begins to work for you, instead of against you. Time begins to work for you, instead of against you. Before you know it, it becomes unthinkable to move backward; it's just not you anymore. You left the old you behind so long ago, that you no longer remember the urges that made you do the things you did.

I've been working on my wish for a long time, and I'm starting to lose faith. What can I do?

As a rule of thumb, success will take longer than you think. Everything worthwhile in life seems to take longer than we want it to. That's one reason so many people feel like failures. They lose patience. They become discouraged. They give up. But the problem isn't their lack of progress, it is their unrealistic expectations. They expect everything to go according to plan. It won't.

So why bother to plan? Because a plan focuses your energy and your efforts toward your objective. That doesn't mean everything will happen the way you want it to, or in the time frame you want, but it does mean that you will be moving toward your objective. If you keep working toward it, ultimately you will succeed. But you have to give it time—whatever time it takes.

Resources

In writing *The Magic Lamp,* I've borrowed freely from dozens of books and tapes I've come across during the past two decades. The short list that follows is the best of these resources, organized by category, so you can pinpoint the works most likely to help you acquire or master the skills you need to make your wishes come true.

Achievement

Fritz, Robert. *The Path of Least Resistance.* Salem, MA: Stillpoint Publishing.

This book provides valuable insight into the power and process of making choices.

The Neuropsychology of Achievement. Pleasanton, CA: Sybervision. Audiocassette album.

A useful set of cassettes about how you can "wire" your brain for achievement. The material is excellent; the delivery by a professional narrator less so; it lacks the presence and passion of the person who actually developed the ideas.

Robbins, Anthony. *Awake the Giant Within*. New York: Summit Books.

> Robbins blends his version of NLP (Neurolinguistic Programming) with unique insights into personal development. *Giant* provides one of the most complete and detailed guides available for making the changes you want to make in your own life.

Sher, Barbara, with Annie Gottlieb. *Wishcraft*. New York: Ballantine.

> A highly readable and down-to-earth look at how to get what you want from life. Sher and Gottlieb offer particularly useful information about how to make plans, how to schedule those plans, and how to get help from other people in making your dreams come true.

Creativity

Keil, John M. *The Creative Mystique: How to Manage It, Nurture It, and Make It Pay*. New York: Wiley Sound Business. Audiocassette.

> A brief and useful program about how you can tap your creativity to improve your life.

Vance, Mike. *Creative Thinking*. Niles, IL: Nightingale-Conant. Audiocassette album.

> If you think creativity is something you're either born with or not, you're half right—everyone is born with it. But most of us don't know how to put it to use. This audiocassette album shows you the way.

Happiness

Canfield, Jack, and Mark Victor Hansen. *Chicken Soup for the Soul: 101 Stories to Open the Heart and Rekindle the Spirit*. Deerfield Beach, FL: Health Communications, Inc.

> If you like inspirational stories, you'll treasure this delightful collection of them.

Covey, Stephen R., A. Roger Merrill, and Rebecca R. Merrill. *First Things First*, New York: Simon & Schuster.

> This is a "must read" because it speaks to the heart of finding happiness amid the stresses and strains of modern living. The theme is captured in the title: If you concentrate on the most important things first, your life will unfold like the miracle it really is. The problem, for most of us, is that we put first things last. Rarely do we take the time to figure out what is important to us. Or if we do figure it out, we put it off in the name of so called "urgent" tasks that demand immediate attention (but may not be worth doing). If you want to find out how to set your life on it's proper course and keep it there, this is the book to read.

Csikszentmihaly, Mihaly. *Flow: The Psychology of Optimal Experience*. New York: Harper Perennial.

> Another "must read." If you've ever had one of those moments when you felt on top of the world, you'll love this book because it explains how you got there and how you can get back. This isn't just a good book, it's an important book. It does a remarkably good job of performing an almost impossible task: explaining the mystery of happiness and showing you how to achieve it.

Csikszentmihaly, Mihaly. *The Evolving Self: A Psychology for the Third Millennium*. New York: Harper Perennial.

> This wonderful book reviews and refines the insights contained in *Flow* (see above) and develops them into a powerful model for how to live a life that maximizes joy, fulfillment, and happiness.

Frankl, Victor E. *Man's Search for Meaning: An Introduction to Logotherapy*. New York: Touchstone.

> "Meaning" is the most common denominator among the various philosophies of happiness. Where people find meaning, they usually find happiness. In this moving and profound book, Dr. Frankl shows how human beings can find meaning where they least expect it, even under the most oppressive of circumstances. As a backdrop for this theme, he relates his own experiences as an inmate in the Nazi death camps during World War II.

Peck, M. Scott, M.D. *The Road Less Traveled*. New York: Touchstone.

> A "must read"—one of those rare books that makes you a better person simply from having read it. You learn about psychology, about yourself, and about how to live the kind of life that both rewards you and fulfills you—and leaves the world a better place.

Getting Published

Appelbaum, Judith. *How to Get Happily Published*. Fourth Edition. New York: Harper Perennial.

> If you think getting a book published is a mystery, here's the book that will demystify the process for you. Not only does it show you how to go about

finding an agent and a publisher, but it also shows how to promote the book when it's published. You'll even learn how to publish a book yourself.

Herman, Jeff. *Insider's Guide to Book Editors, Publishers, and Literary Agents*, Rocklin, CA: Prima Publishing.

How do you find an agent and a publisher? This book will show you how. It's the only source I know that identifies key people in publishing firms and agencies, along with their special areas of interest, so that you can contact the people who are most likely to be interested in what you've written.

Nicholas, Ted, *How to Publish a Book and Sell a Million Copies*, Enterprise•Dearborn Publishing.

If you've already decided to publish a book yourself (or if you're considering it), this book will show you how to go about it and how to market it after you publish it.

Poynter, Dan. *The Self-Publishing Manual: How to Write, Print, and Sell Your Own Book*. Santa Barbara, CA: Para Publishing.

If you'd like to see your name on the cover of a book, read this one. It contains more good and useful information about self-publishing than any other single source I've read.

Leadership

Blanchard, Kenneth, Ph.D., and Spencer Johnson, M.D. *The One-Minute Manager*. New York: William Morrow and Company.

A phenomenal success when it came out more than a decade ago, this little book is still setting sales records, and with good reason. If you want to learn some of the most important principles for successfully managing people, this is a great place to start.

Covey, Stephen R. *Principle Centered Leadership*, Niles, IL: Nightingale-Conant. Audiocassette album.

An excellent program that applies Covey's ideas about principle-centered living to help solve the problems of leadership.

Learning

Zinsser, William. *Writing to Learn*, New York: HarperCollins.

The old saw tells us that if we want to learn something, we need to teach it. Zinsser shows us another way: If we want to learn something, we need to write about it.

Memory

Lorayne, Harry, and Jerry Lucas. *The Memory Book*. New York: Ballantine Books.

Everyone is born with a terrific memory, but only the lucky few ever learn how to use it. This book shows how you can become one of them. If you would like to develop your ability to remember names, facts, and other information, this book will help you do it.

Trudeau, Kevin. *Mega Memory*. New York: American Memory Institute. Audiocassette album.

This cassette album will help you remember anything you want, from names to faces to facts. If you would like to have a better memory—but think you weren't "born with it"—think again, and listen to these tapes.

Negotiating

Dawson, Roger. *Power Negotiating*. Niles, IL: Nightingale-Conant. Audiocassette album.

> This excellent audio program is full of rock-solid techniques for negotiating toward a win-win agreement.

Fisher, Roger and William Ury. *Getting to Yes*. New York: Penguin Books.

> Whatever you choose to accomplish chances are you're going to have to work with other people to make it happen. And chances are their needs are going to be different from your own. To turn opponents into supporters, you have to learn to negotiate what the experts call a "win-win" agreement. This short book is one of the most straightforward and widely read guides for doing just that.

Jandt, Fred E., with Paul Gillette. *Win-Win Negotiating: Turning Conflict into Agreement*. New York: Wiley Sound Business. Audiocassette.

> This is a shorter (and cheaper) audiocassette program, that provides a good introduction to the principles of effective negotiation.

Neurolinguistic Programming

Bandler, Richard, and John Grinder. *The Structure of Magic*. Vols. 1 and 2. Palo Alto, CA: Science and Behavior Books, Inc.

> The men who gave us neurolinguistic programming (NLP), Richard Bandler and John Grinder, set out originally to create a method by which anyone could model and then master any skill—what you might call a science of human

achievement. Their efforts produced one of the most elegant and powerful models of human communication.

This model for modeling sheds new and welcome light on how we communicate with ourselves (to learn new behavior, for example), and how we communicate with others. During the past two decades, NLP has influenced many disciplines, including education, psychotherapy, sports, business, and sales.

These two volumes are the first that Bandler and Grinder published about their research. They're dry and difficult reading, and they're brilliant. If you want to understand where NLP came from, read them. If you simply want to understand how NLP can be of use to you, read *Unlimited Power* (below).

Robbins, Anthony. *Unlimited Power*. New York: Simon & Schuster.

A "must read" as the book that brought NLP to a mass audience. As a blueprint for achievement and success, it remains unequaled. Robbins combines some of the most powerful techniques from NLP with his own useful and profound insights into human nature. He provides a readable, entertaining, and invaluable guide to making the most of your life.

Persuasion

Carnegie, Dale. *How to Win Friends and Influence People*. New York: Pocket Books.

If you don't count ancient scripture, this is the best book there is about how to get along with other people.

Cialdini, Robert B., Ph.D. *Influence: The New Psychology of Persuasion*. New York: Quill.

You would be amazed at how often each day you are influenced in ways that you would never dream about. You would also be amazed at how easy it is to become a more powerful influencer yourself. If you would like to master the skills of persuasion and influence, this book is a superb tool to help you do it.

Problem Solving

Gibson, Bill. *The Art and Science of Problem Solving*. Niles, IL: Nightingale-Conant. Audiocassette album.

Don't wish for fewer problems, wish for more skills to solve them. This cassette album is a good place to start. It gives you a wealth of techniques and exercises to develop your innate problem-solving ability.

Self-Image

Branden, Nathaniel. *Succeeding Through Inner Strength*. Niles, IL: Nightingale-Conant. Audiocassette album.

If you find yourself wishing for the strength to face a great challenge, you'll find these tapes a wonderful catalyst for building that strength. Full of wisdom, humanity, and practical advice, Branden's program helps you develop self-esteem at the same time you're developing intestinal fortitude.

Canfield, Jack. *How to Have High Self-Esteem*, Niles, IL: Nightingale-Conant. Audiocassette album.

Having low self-esteem is like swimming upstream backward. There are very few problems on this planet that aren't in some way connected to low self-

esteem, either your own, or someone else's. You can't do much about someone else's self-esteem, but you can do yours a world of good. Canfield will
show you how.

Selling

Miller, Robert B., Steven E. Heiman, with Tad Tuleja. *Strategic Selling*. New York:
Warner Books.

> If you're in the business of making complex sales (in other words, in each
> account you have to persuade more than one person to buy before you make
> a sale), and you want to make yourself as close to unbeatable as a salesperson
> can get, read this book as well as the two below.

Rackham, Neil. *Major Account Sales Strategy*. New York: McGraw-Hill.

> If you sell to major accounts and you're looking for a competitive edge, read
> this book.

Rackham, Neil. *SPIN Selling*. New York: McGraw-Hill.

> If you're in sales and you're looking for a competitive edge, read this book.

Self-Discipline

Neuropsychology of Self-Discipline. Pleasanton, CA: Sybervision. Audiocassette
album.

> This audiocassette album shows you how to use the advanced learning tech-
> niques developed by neuroscientist Karl Pribram to master self-discipline.

The content is superb; the narration is done by a professional, rather than by Dr. Pribram himself, so you lose something in the translation (but it's still an excellent program).

Sleep

Bourke, Dale Hanson. *The Sleep Management Plan*. New York: Harper Paperbacks.

If you would like to spend less time sleeping and more time doing what you wish, this book can show you how. (Remember to consult your physician before you start messing around with your sleeping habits.)

Speaking

Anthony, Robert, Ph.D. *Put Your Money Where Your Mouth Is: How to Make a Fortune in Public Speaking*. New York: Berkley Books.

If you've ever fantasized about earning a living as an "expert," jetting around the country, staying in fancy hotels, and being paid a lot of money to talk about things that interest you, it doesn't have to be a fantasy. Dr. Anthony's book shows you how to make that kind of dream come true.

Cooper, Dr. Morton. *Change Your Voice, Change Your Life*. New York: Harper & Row.

Your voice has a great deal to do with how other people respond to you. This book shows how you've chosen the voice you have, and how you can choose to modify that voice to make yourself a more effective communicator.

Frank, Milo O. *How to Get Your Point Across in 30 Seconds—Or Less*. New York: Simon & Schuster.

If you can't make your point in under 30 seconds, you don't understand what you're trying to say. If you don't understand what you're trying to say, how can anyone else? Frank shows you how to distill even a complex idea into something you can communicate in less time than it takes the average person to tune you out.

Nightingale, Earl. *Public Speaking*. Niles, IL: Nightingale-Conant. Audiocassette album.

This audiocassette program shares with you the insights that helped make self-improvement philospher Earl Nightingale one of the most admired and requested speakers in the country.

Walters, Dottie and Lillett. *Speak and Grow Rich*. New York: Prentice-Hall.

If you're serious about becoming a professional speaker, this is the first and best book to read.

Success

Chopra, Deepak. *The Seven Spiritual Laws of Success*. San Rafael, CA: Amber-Allen Publishing and New World Library.

Deepak Chopra is both a medical doctor, trained in the latest technologies of modern healing, and a practitioner of Ayurvedic medicine, handed down from ancient India. With his unique grasp of what is useful from the East and from the West, from the new and from the old, he dispenses profound insights as matter-of-factly as the rest of us might talk about the latest sports scores or our favorite TV show. This little book (116 pages) is a wise and gentle introduction to the spiritual principles that underlie a successful life.

Covey, Stephen R. *The Seven Habits of Highly Successful People*. New York: Simon & Schuster.

> Covey has a way of putting his finger on the most important issues facing those who wish to live a successful and fulfilling life. *The Seven Habits* shows you how to reap the rewards of a life based on principle, character, and a commitment to conscience.

Hill, Napoleon. *Think and Grow Rich*. New York: Fawcett.

> This is the book that spawned the self-help movement. It wasn't the first self-help book, to be sure, but it was the one that caught fire and the one that almost everybody else in the business quotes. This is the book in which Earl Nightingale first read the words that he later made famous in *The Strangest Secret* ("You are what you think about"). This is the book that for many of today's leading self-help thinkers served as their introduction to the fundamentals of success.

Nightingale, Earl. *The Essence of Success*. Niles, IL: Nightingale-Conant. Series of audiocassette albums.

> Earl Nightingale's *The Strangest Secret*, recorded in the 1950s, was the first self-help album to sell a million copies. He devoted his life to studying success and achievement, and then sharing with others what he had learned. What set him apart was that he took the time to master the arts of communication—he was a compelling writer, public speaker, and broadcaster—so that he could better convey the information he had made it his mission to share.
>
> *The Essence of Success* is really the essence of Earl Nightingale. It's a delightful and thought-provoking distillation of thousands of hours of his daily radio programs, audiocassettes, and interviews, worth every moment you invest in listening to it, and every penny you invest in buying a copy for your own library.

Nightingale, Earl. *The New Lead the Field*, Niles, IL: Nightingale-Conant. Audio-cassette album.

> Nightingale recorded dozens of albums and cassette programs, many of them culled from the daily radio broadcasts he made during a career that spanned decades. *The New Lead the Field* was an update of an earlier best-selling album *(Lead the Field)*. It was one of his last full-length programs, and one of his best, filled with wisdom and practical advice about how to make your life everything you've ever wanted it to be.

Nightingale, Earl. *The Strangest Secret*. Niles, IL: Nightingale-Conant. Audiocas-sette album.

> Thirty years after he released the original recording of *The Strangest Secret*, the album that launched an entire industry, Earl Nightingale recorded a full-length audiocassette album with the same title. In it he reviews his original thinking about success and enhances it with insights drawn from an additional three decades of study, experience, and reflection.

Robbins, Anthony. *Personal Power: A 30-Day Program for Unlimited Success*. Irwin-dale, CA: Guthy-Renker Corporation. Series of audiocassette albums.

> There's an old saying that if you want to keep getting the same results, keep doing the same things. But if you want to get different results, you have to do something different. In other words, you have to change. These tapes, perhaps the most powerful curriculum for personal change ever recorded, package the most useful teachings from Mr. Robbins into a 30-day plan to help you firmly set your course on achieving what you've always dreamed about.

Rohn, Jim. *The Art of Exceptional Living*. Niles, IL: Nightingale-Conant. Audio-cassette album.

Ever wonder where inspirational writers get their inspiration? From people like Jim Rohn. This audiocassette album is pithy, useful, and crammed with advice that really can make a difference in your life, and the lives of those you care about.

Sinetar, Marsha. *Do What You Love, The Money Will Follow: Choosing Your Right Livelihood*. New York: Dell.

Sinetar's advice is straight forward: Instead of making your career decisions based on income, make them based on what you want to do with your life. Then the money will follow. She's right, and she offers more than just a lofty ideal. She provides a good strategy and solid advice about how to find your life's work and then make it pay.

Thinking

De Bono, Edward. *The Power of Focused Thinking*. Mamaroneck, NY: International Center for Creative Thinking. Audiocassette album.

Most of us have never learned how to think. We just do what comes naturally to us, without trying to do it better, or do it right. But De Bono has devoted his career to studying the nature of thinking and to communicating his insights to the rest of us so that we can get the most out of our mental abilities. The material in this album is excellent, even though it is performed by a professional narrator, rather than by the author himself.

Time Management

Lakein, Alan. *How to Get Control of Your Time and Your Life*. New York: Signet.

> This is one of the best and most widely read books about how to make the most of your time. If you don't have the time to read this book, boy, do you need it.

Mackenzie, R. Alec. *Time for Success: A Goal-setter's Strategy*, New York: McGraw-Hill.

> Mackenzie, one of the most respected experts in the field of time management, presents a solid strategy for how to put your time to the most effective use.

Writing

Kilpatrick, James J. *The Writer's Art*. Kansas City, MO: Andrews and McMeel.

> Kilpatrick's book is a joy to read. His writing is a stroll through a garden of fresh metaphor. With examples, and by example, he shows you how to add snap, crackle, and pop to whatever you wish to say. Equally rewarding, and unique in what I've read, is the stress on the importance of cadence to good writing. Kilpatrick provides helpful examples from the writings of others, but none are as enlightening as his own rhythmic prose.

Strunk, William Jr., and E. B. White. *The Elements of Style*. New York: Mac-Millan Co.

> Someone once said that every writer should read this book at least once a year. You don't have to be a professional writer to benefit. Anyone who puts words to paper would do well to read this compact, pithy masterpiece.

Zinsser, William. *On Writing Well*. Fifth Edition. New York: HarperCollins.

A "must read." The best advice I ever found about writing, I found in this book. In a couple hundred delightful pages, Zinsser shows you how to write with clarity, simplicity, and humanity—the kind of writing that people will read.

If you write at all—at work, as a hobby, for correspondence—and if you want your readers to comprehend what you're trying to say, I urge you to study this book and practice what it preaches.

Index

About the Author

Keith Ellis is a nationally known speaker, author, columnist, and management consultant whose unique insights about goal setting have made him a guest on leading talk shows across the country.

For twenty-five years he has studied the art and science of human achievement. After graduating magna cum laude from Georgetown University, he became a record-breaking salesperson in the computer industry then worked his way into senior management. In the process, he devoured every book, magazine, and audiocassette he could find about success and human potential, and attended the leading seminars and lectures.

At the age of 28, Mr. Ellis became the chief marketing officer for a multimillion-dollar computer company. At 34, he became president of his own training company, where he created the nationally acclaimed management training seminar, *The Science of Persuasion*™. Today he is president of Keith Ellis Seminars (http://www.selfhelp.com), a firm that specializes in training and consulting on state-of-the-art strategies for peak performance.

Mr. Ellis is the author of *Bootstraps* (http://www.selfhelp.com/bootstraps.html), the first monthly column on the World

About the Author

Wide Web devoted to self-help and self-improvement. His Web site is visited 35,000 times a month from around the world.

For his pioneering thinking, teaching, and leadership in the field of peak performance, Mr. Ellis has been chosen to be listed in both *Who's Who In American Business* and *Who's Who In Media and Communications.*

Speaking Engagements

Keith Ellis has been described as one of the most dynamic and inspirational speakers in the nation. If you are looking for someone to deliver an unforgettable talk or seminar for a special program you're putting together, call Mr. Ellis at 1-800-SET-LAMP. Or contact your favorite speakers bureau.

Mr. Ellis is available for seminars and keynote talks on a number of topics, including:

The Magic of the L.A.M.P.™: *Goal setting for people who hate setting goals.*

The Beginning of Time™: *How to find the time to make your wishes come true.*

Success: GUARANTEED!™: *How To Get Anything You Want from Life.*

Don't just manage—LEAD!™: *How to Get People to Want to Work for You.*

The Lincoln Lessons™: *What Abraham Lincoln can teach us about success.*

The Science of Persuasion™: *How to Maximize Your Influence Without Minimizing Your Integrity.*

True North™: *How to find out who you are and what you are meant to do with your life.*

KEITH ELLIS SEMINARS
1-800-SET-LAMP
(800-738-5267)
magiclamp@selfhelp.com
http://www.selfhelp.com